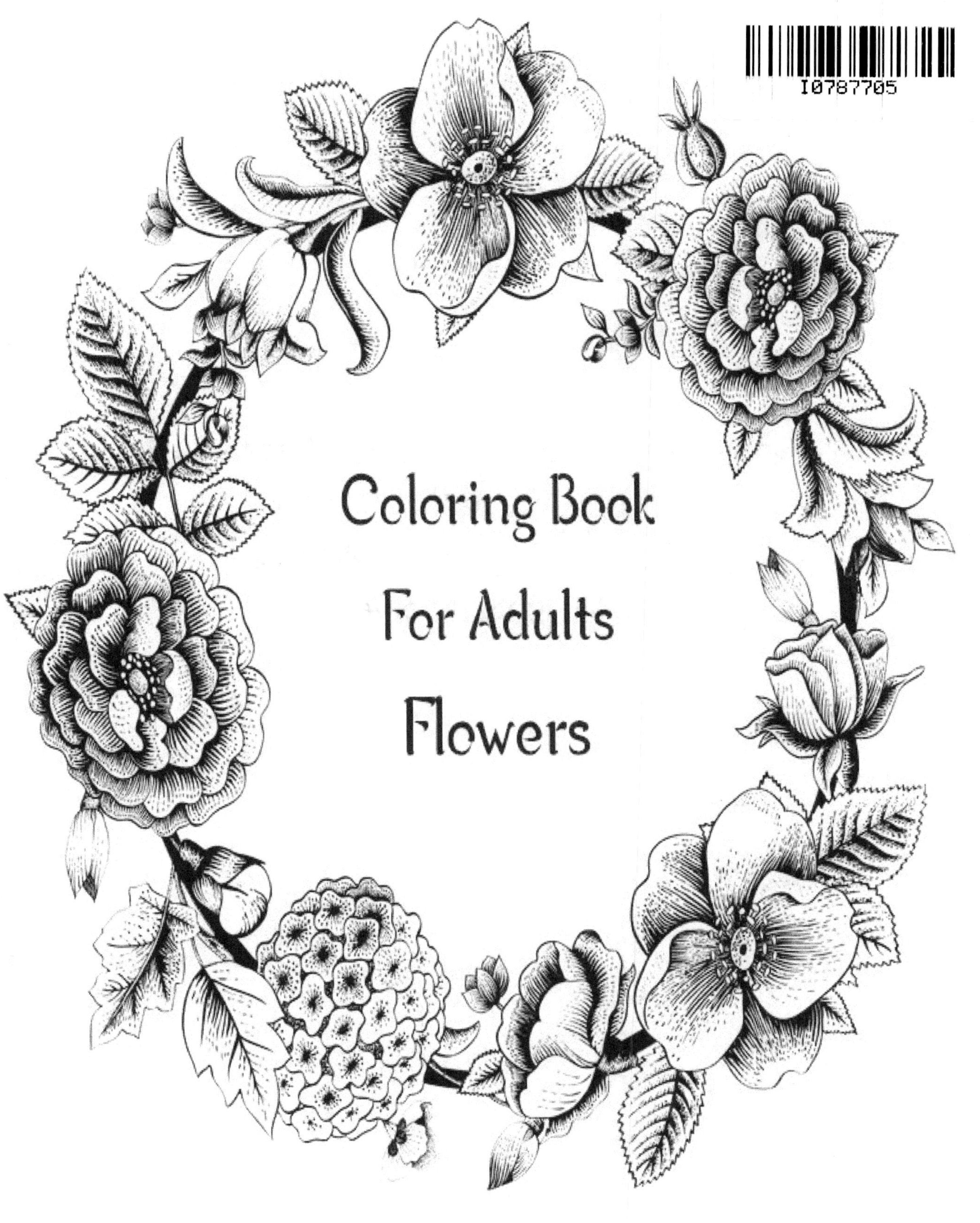

Coloring Book
For Adults
Flowers

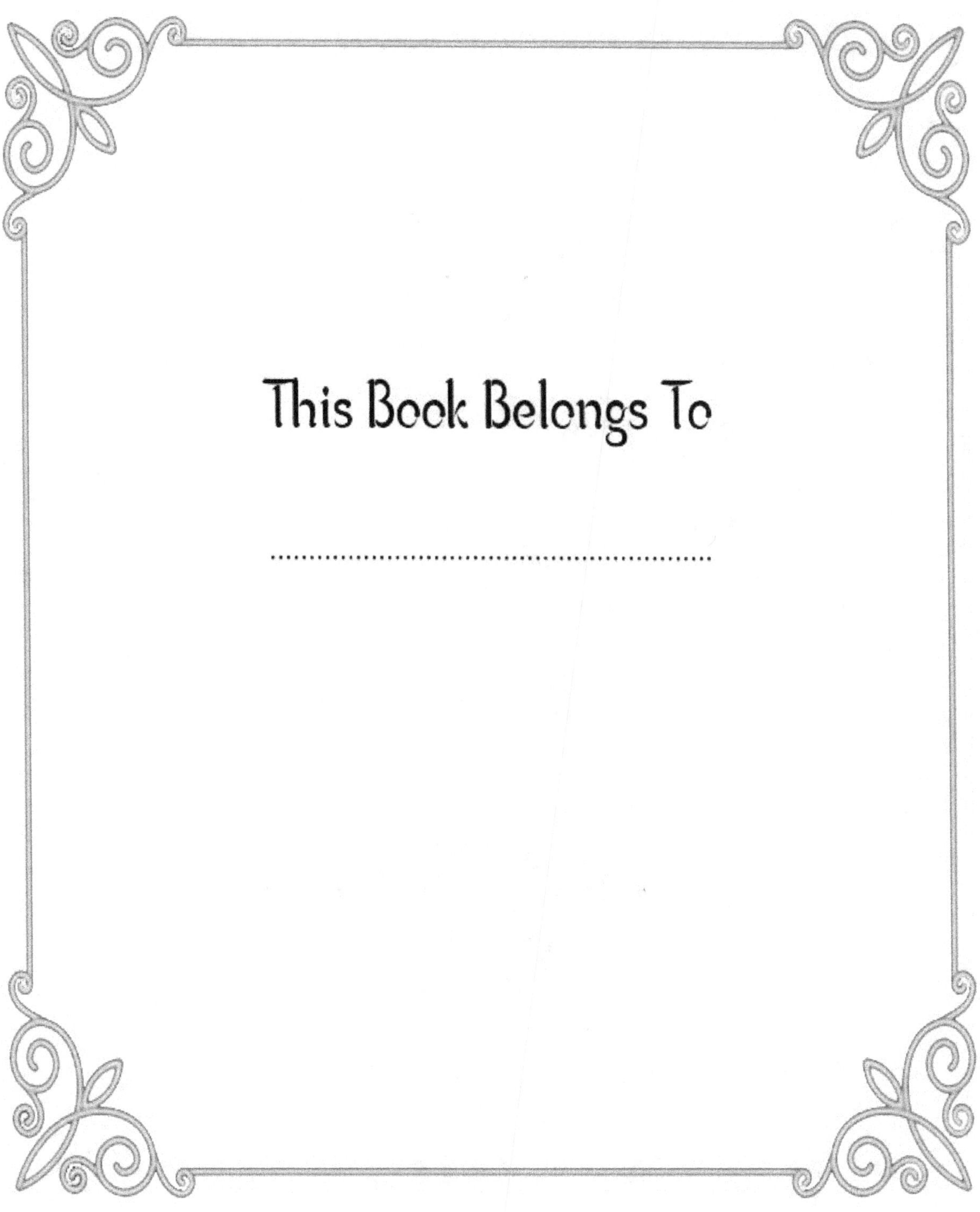

This Book Belongs To

....

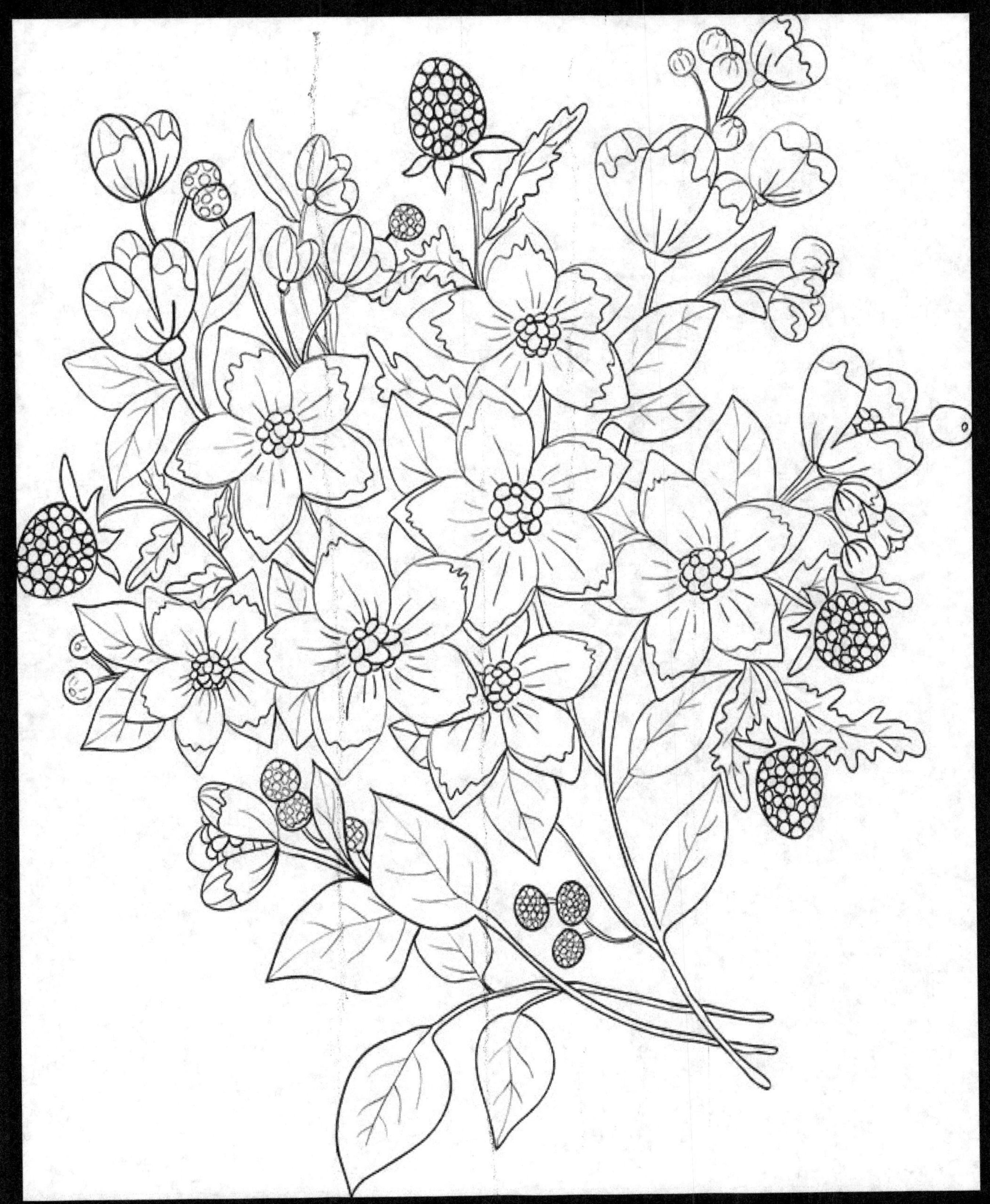

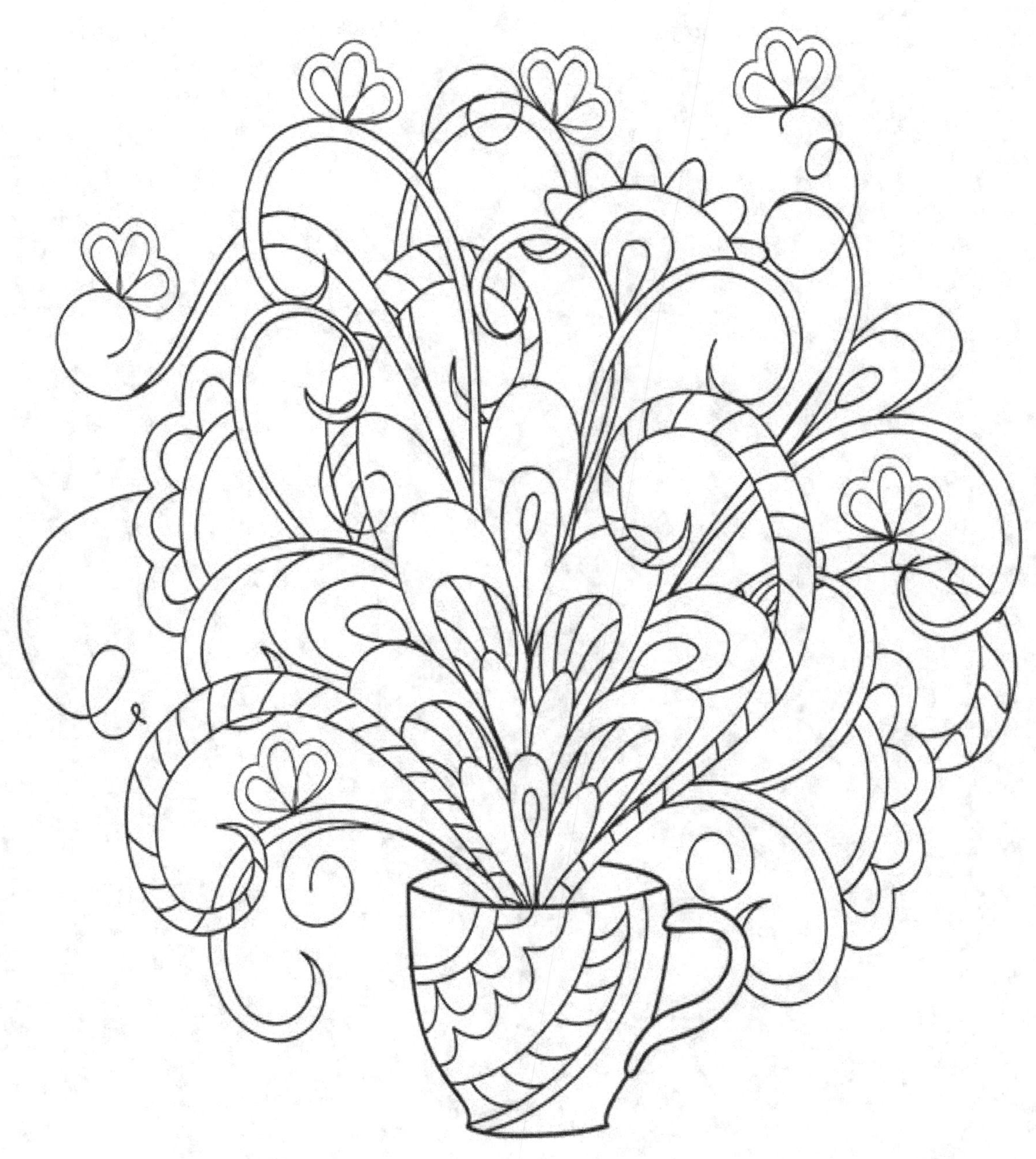

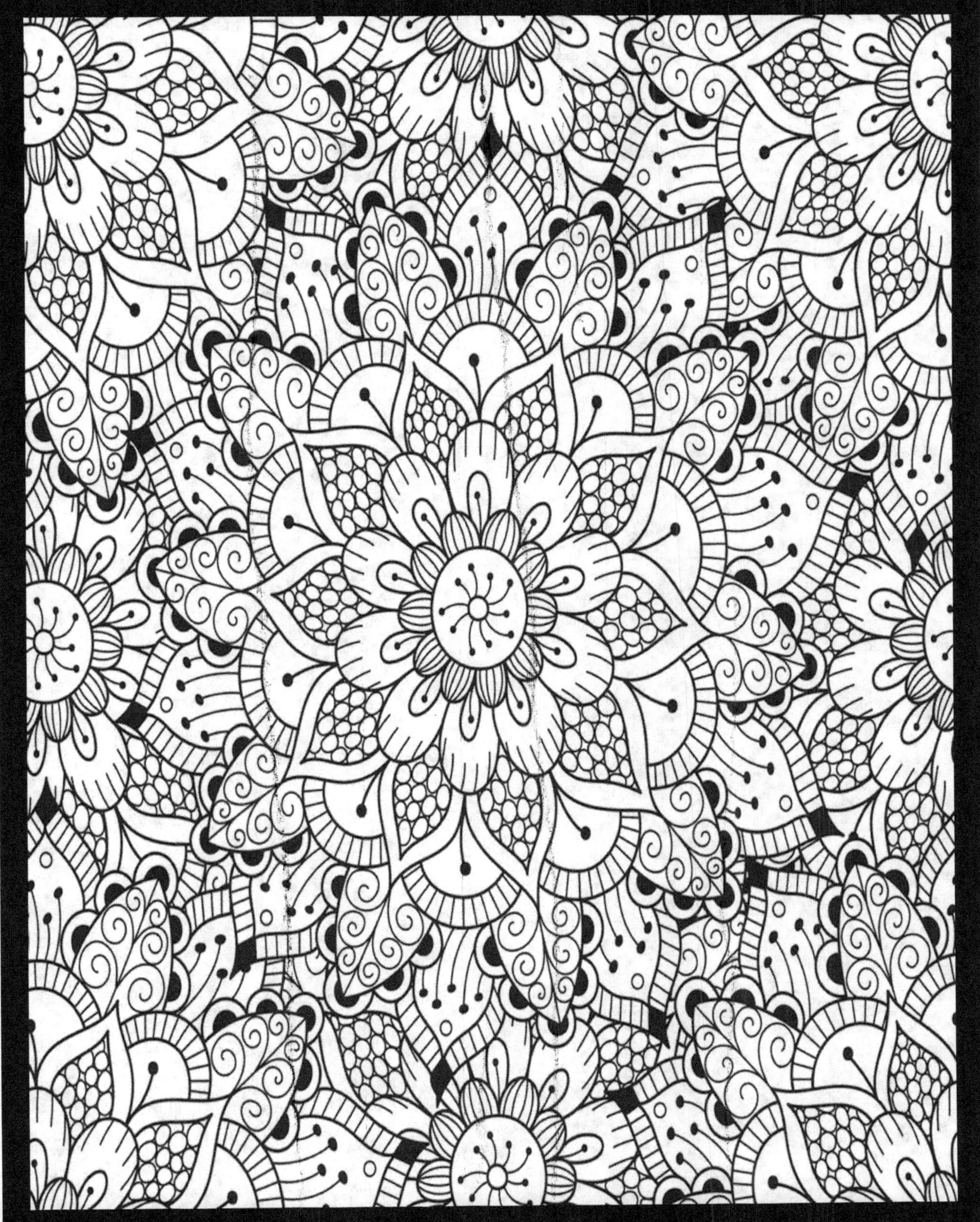

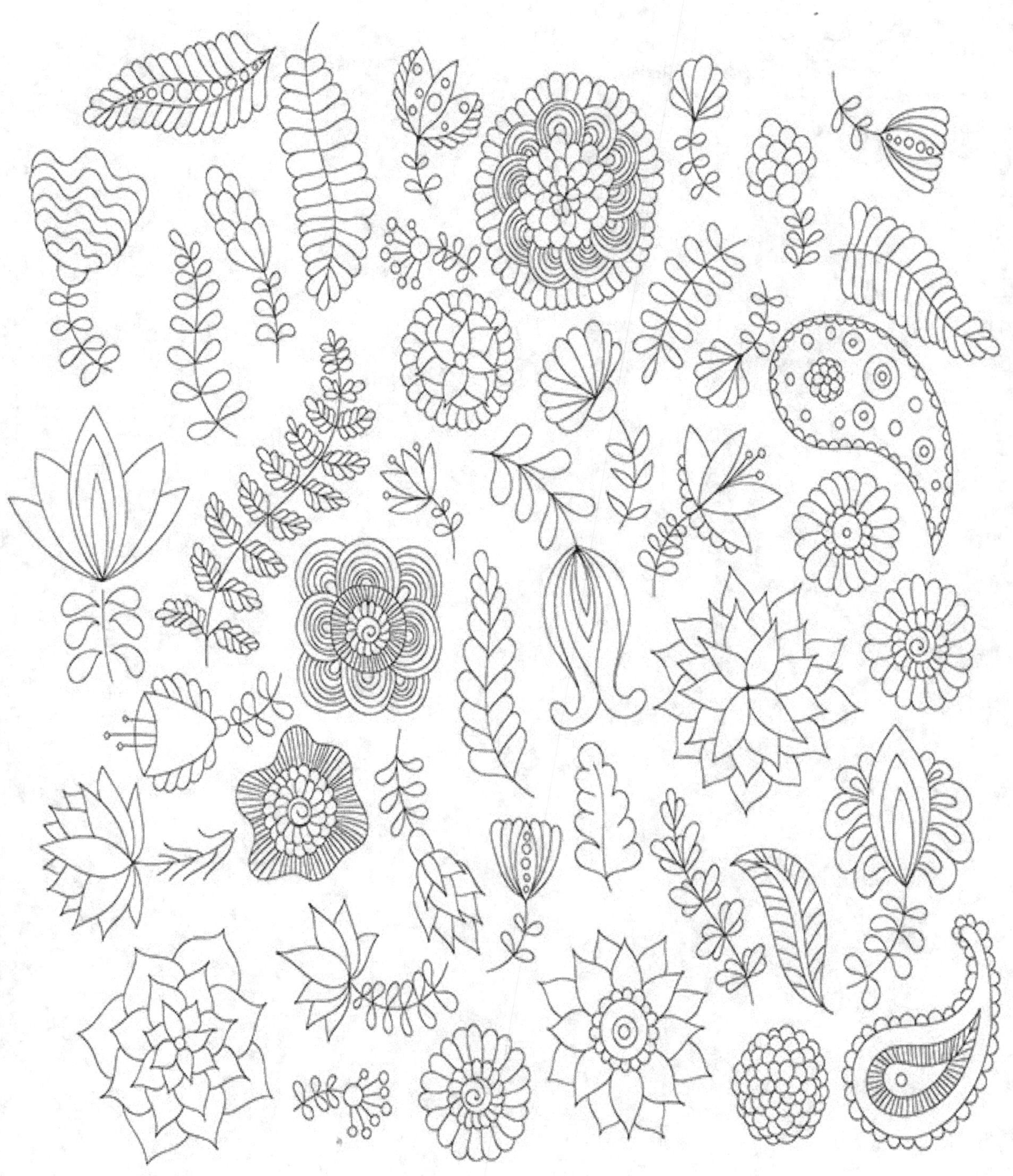

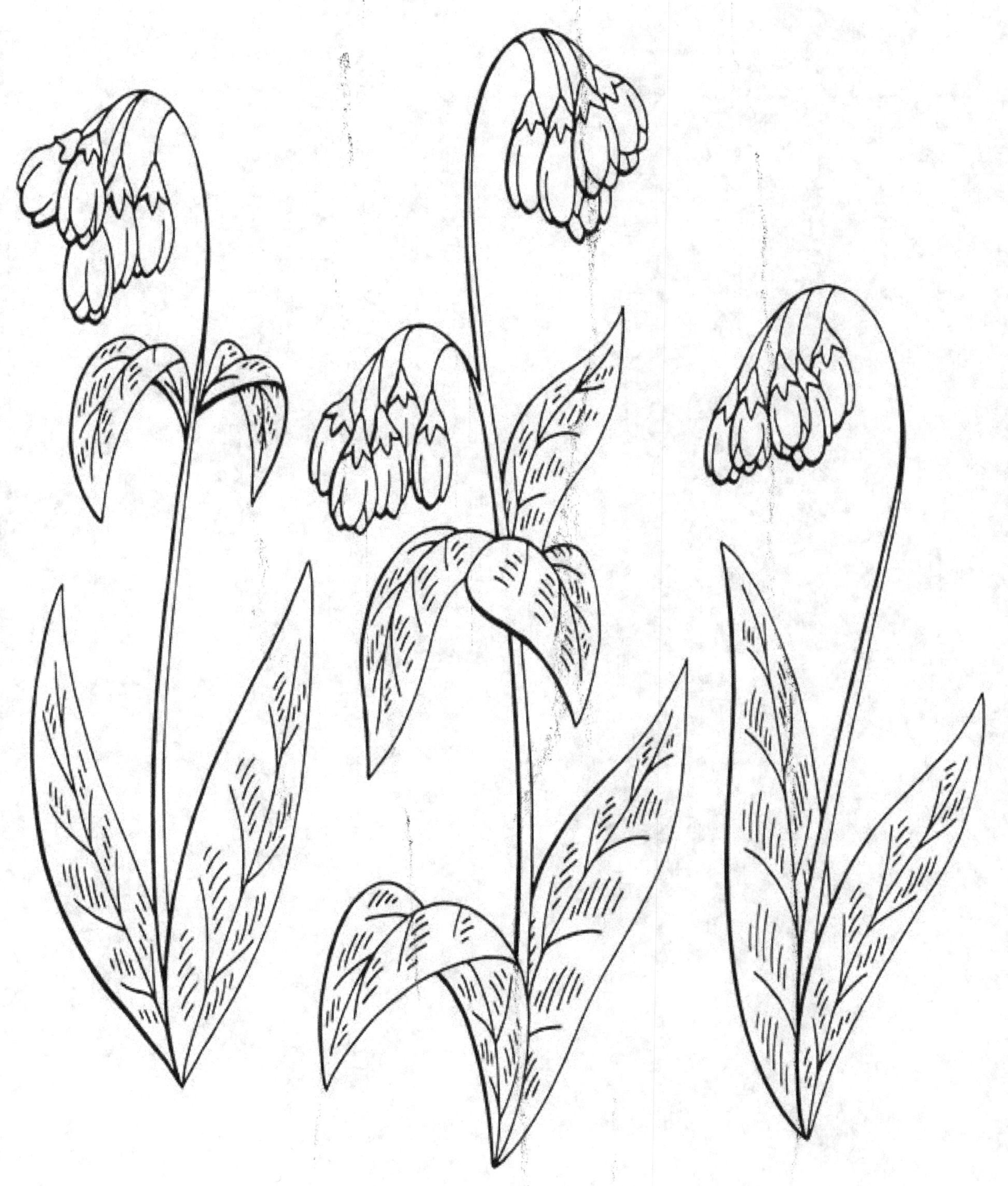

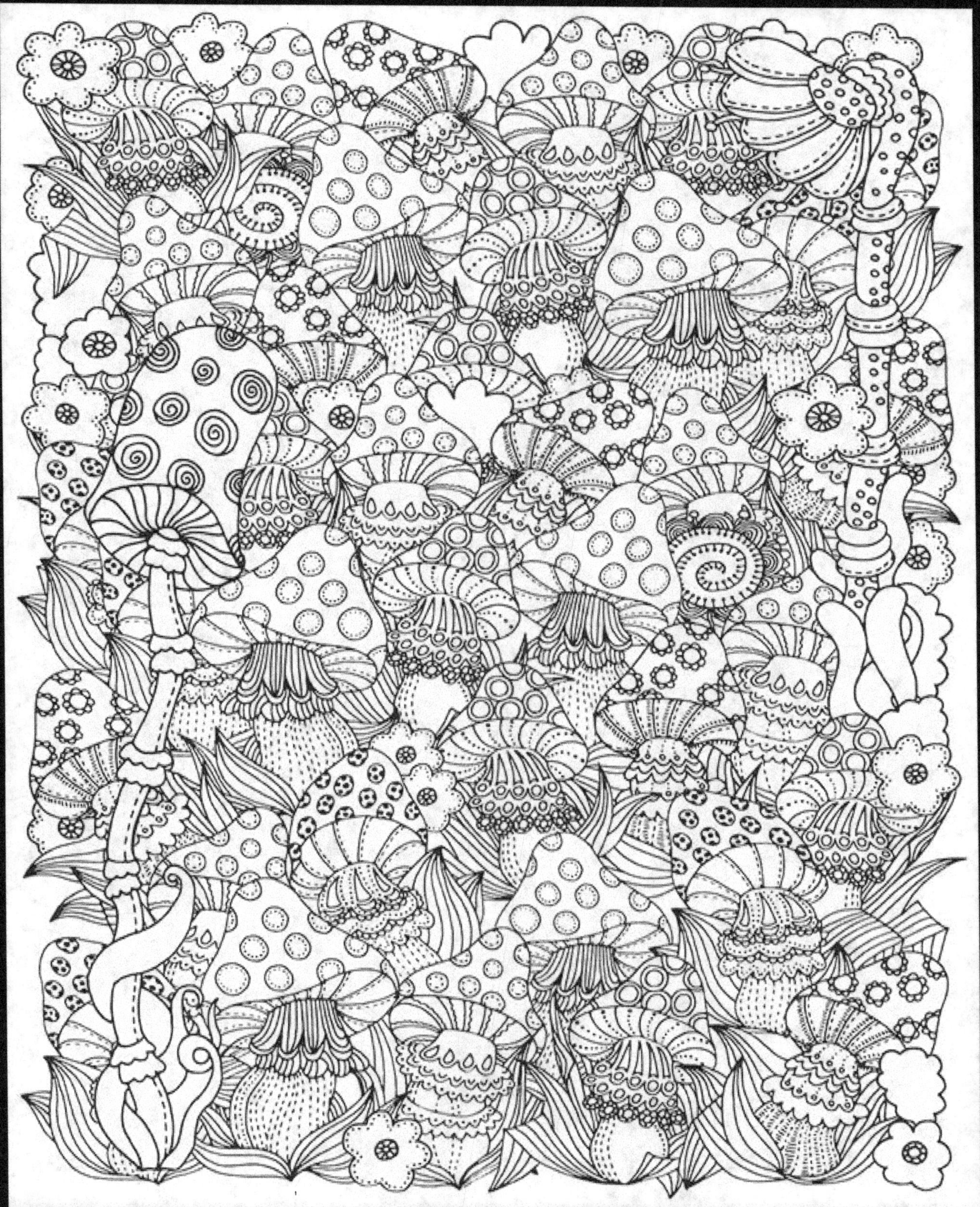

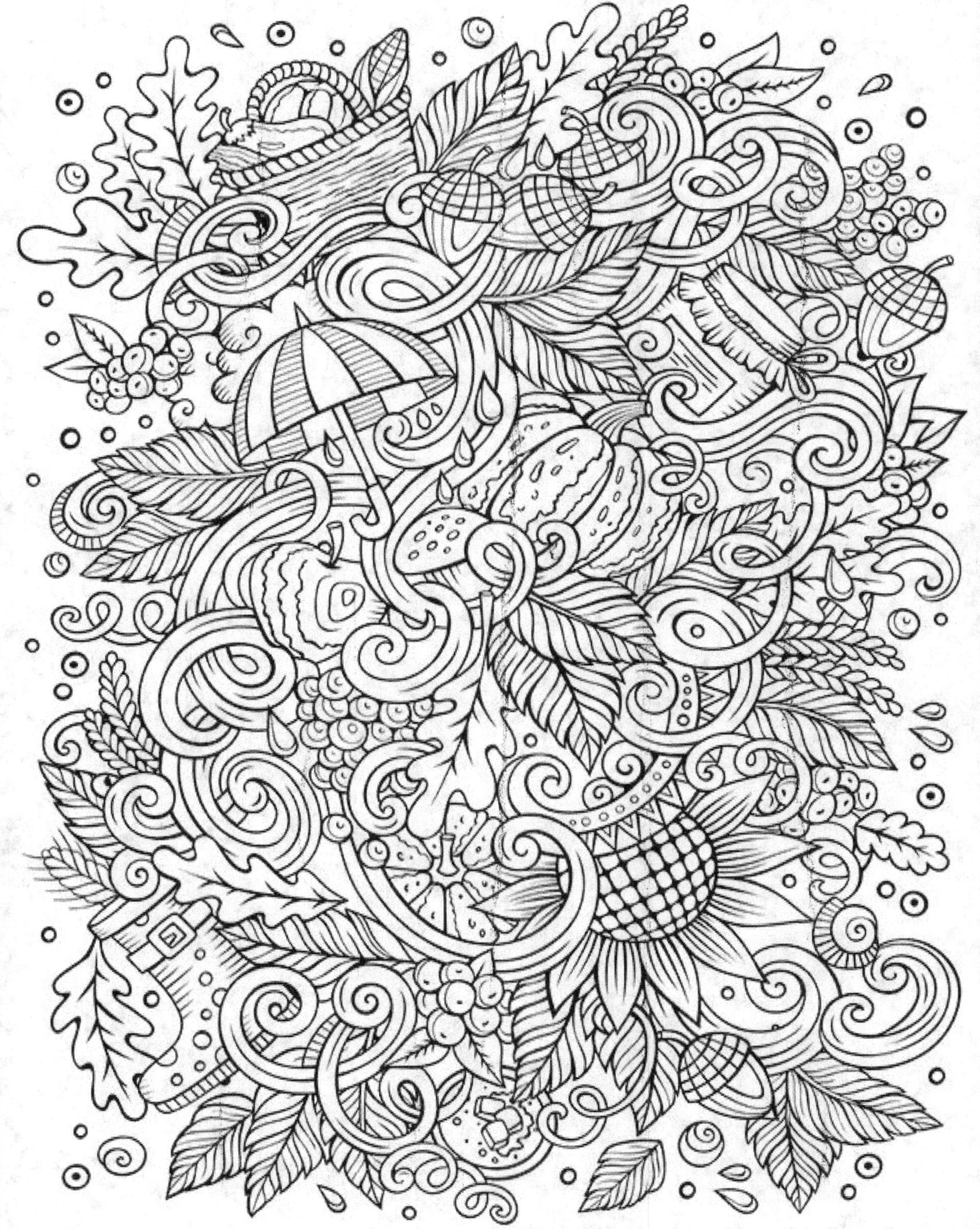

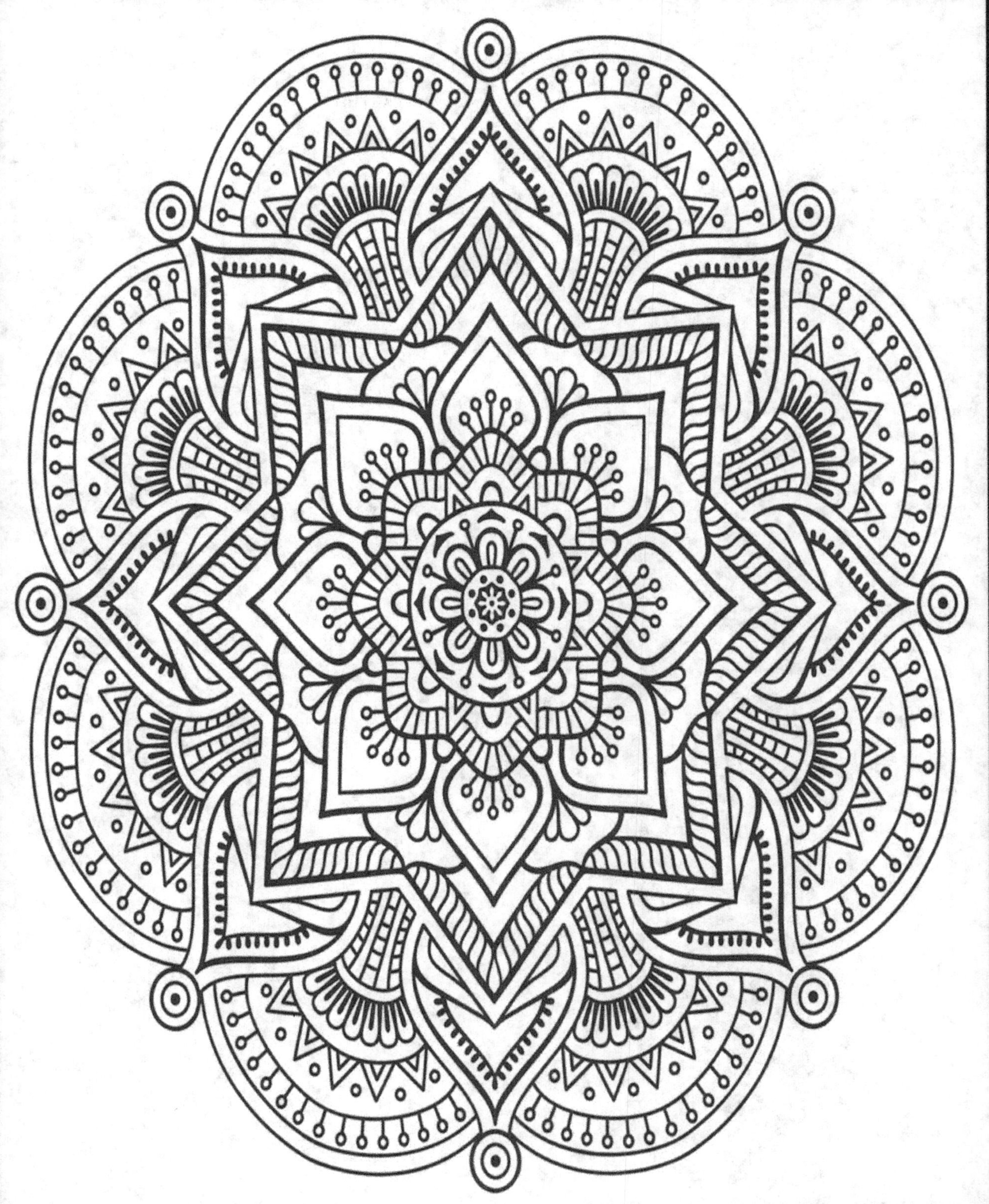

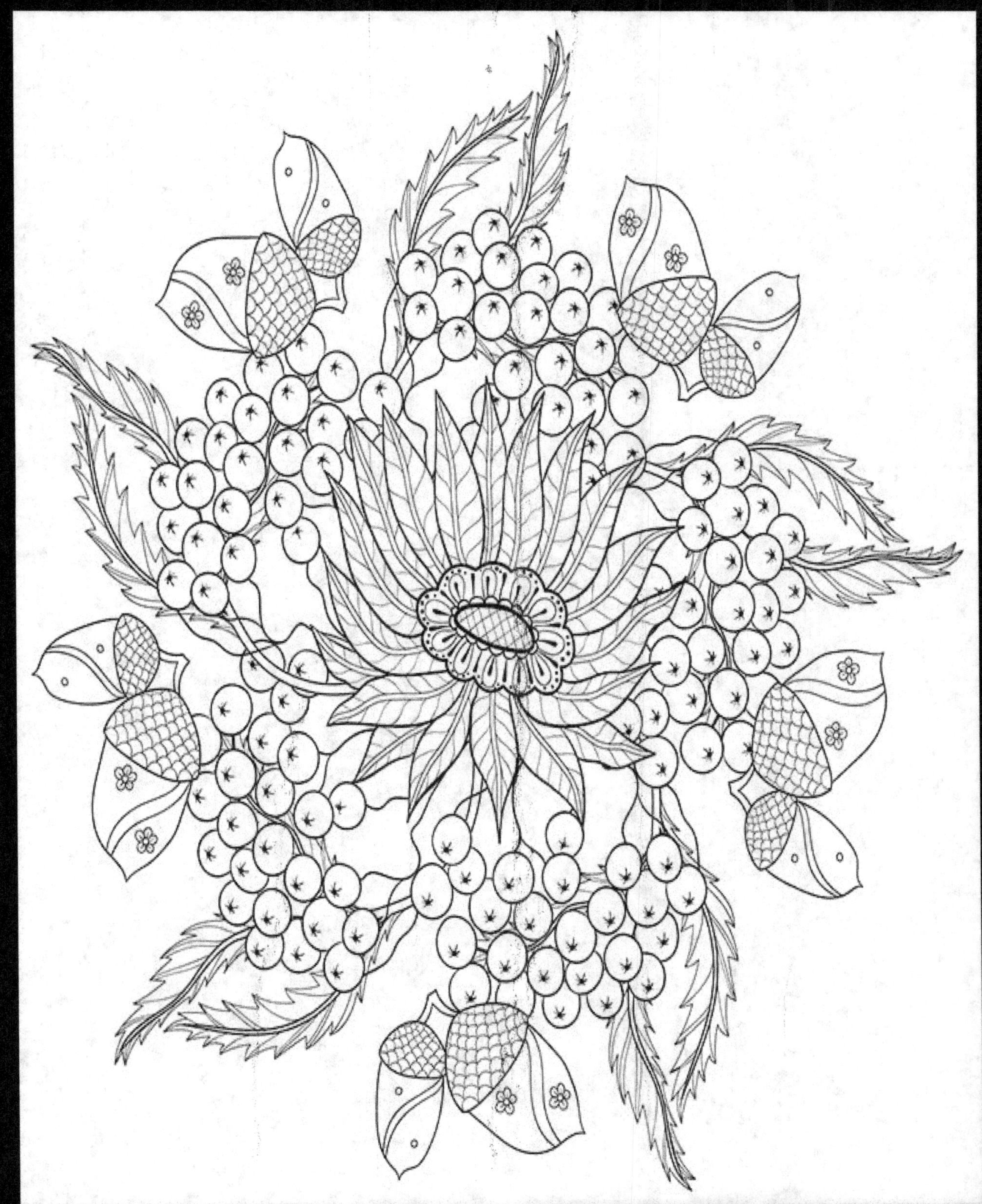

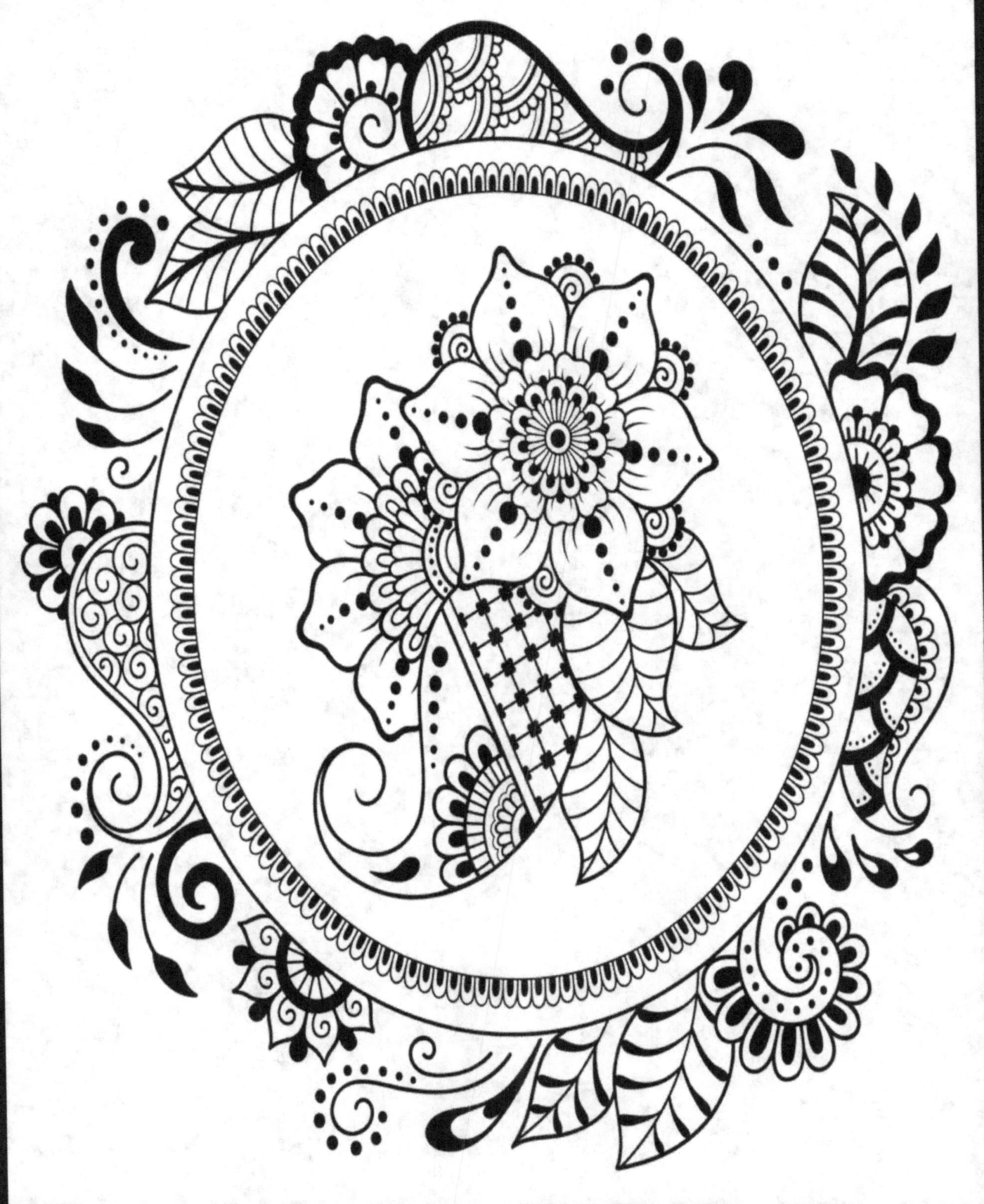

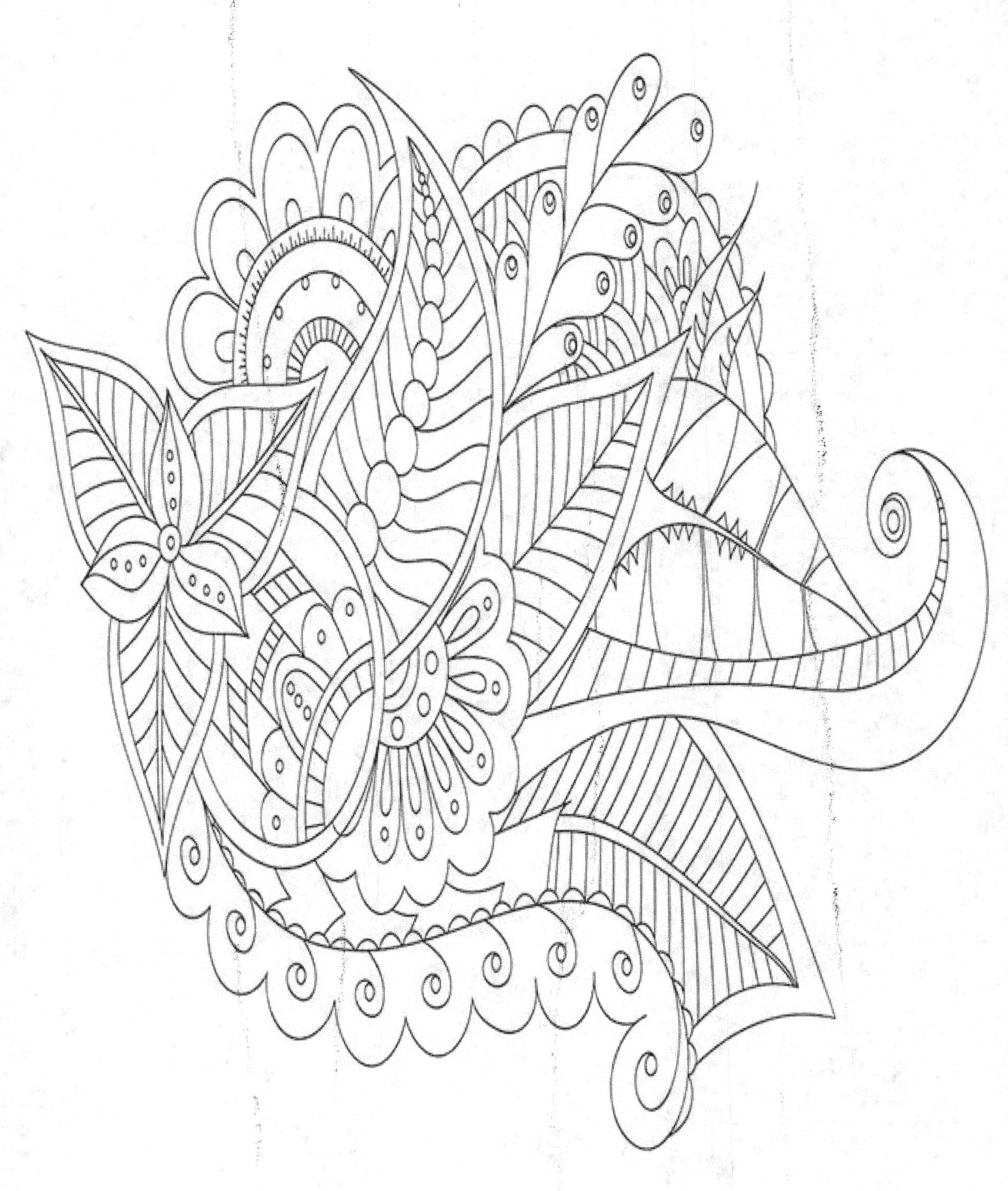

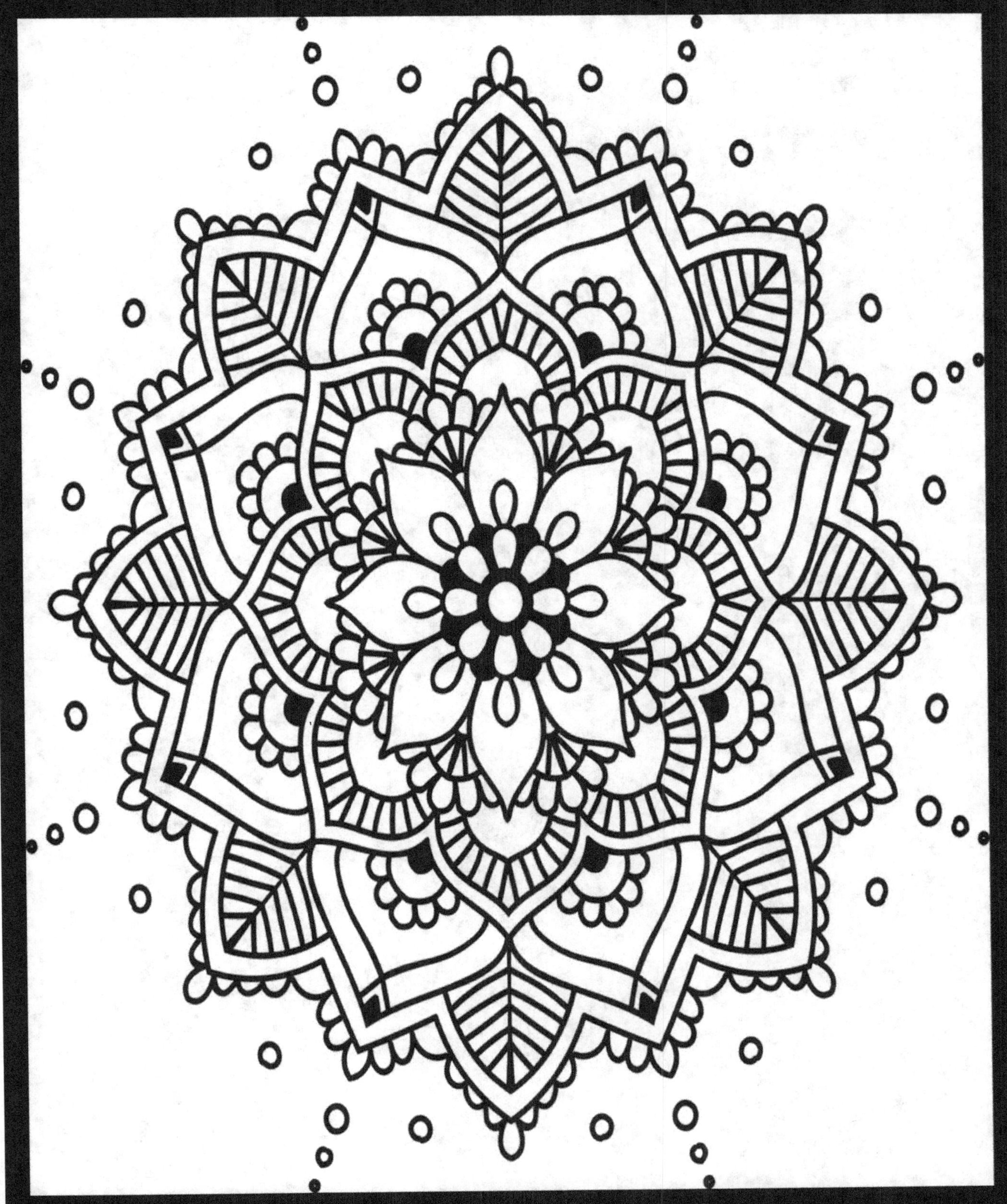

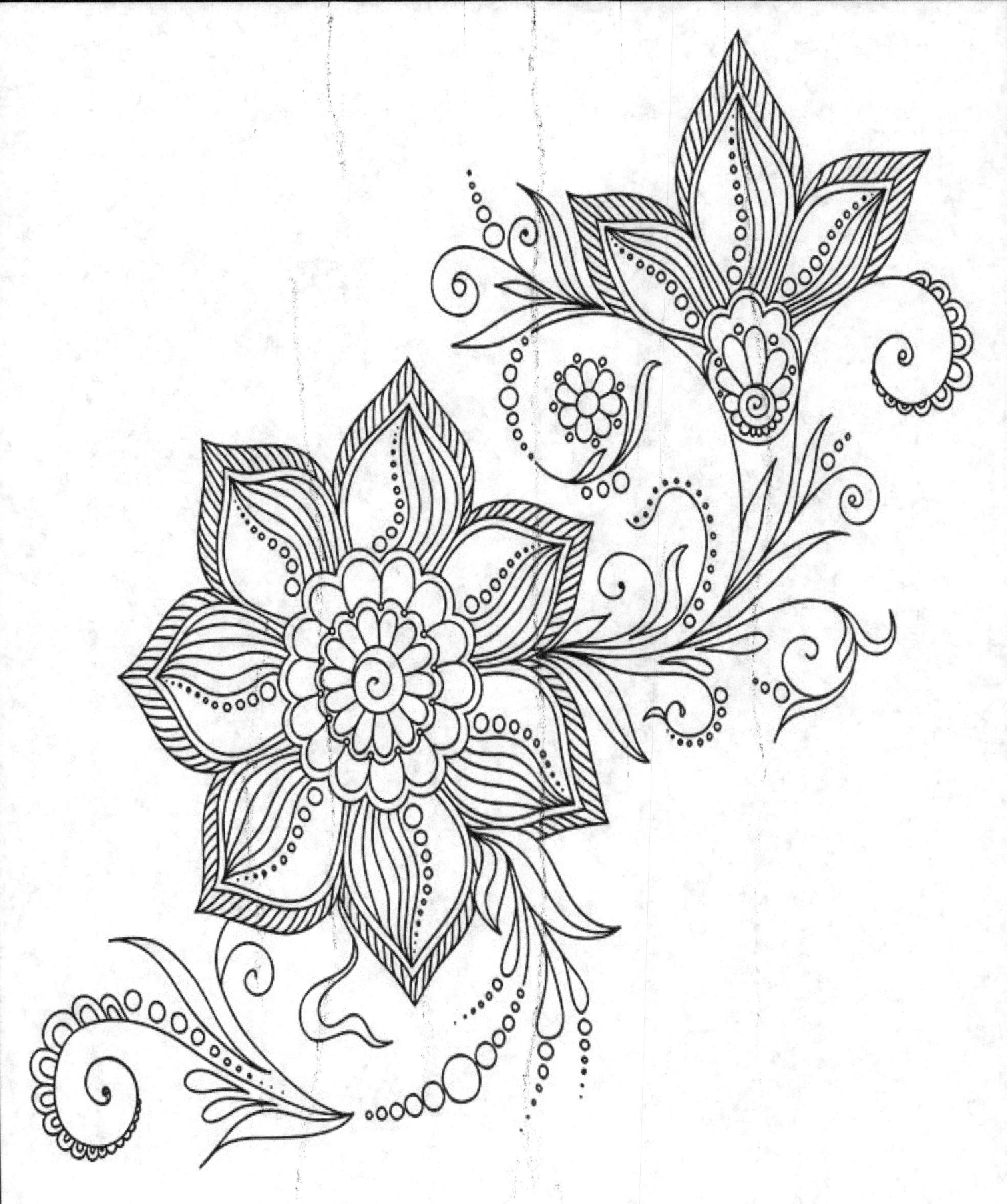

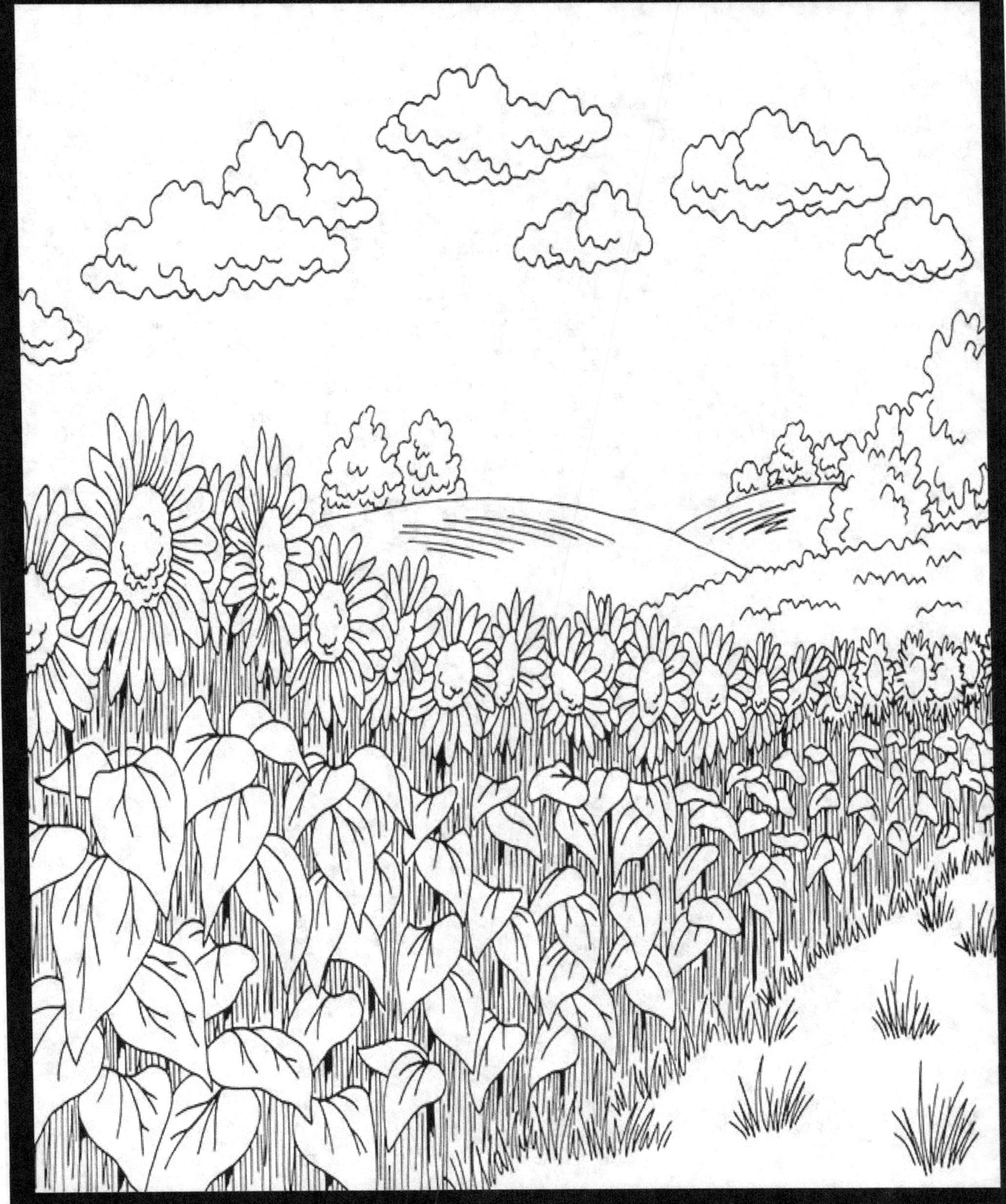

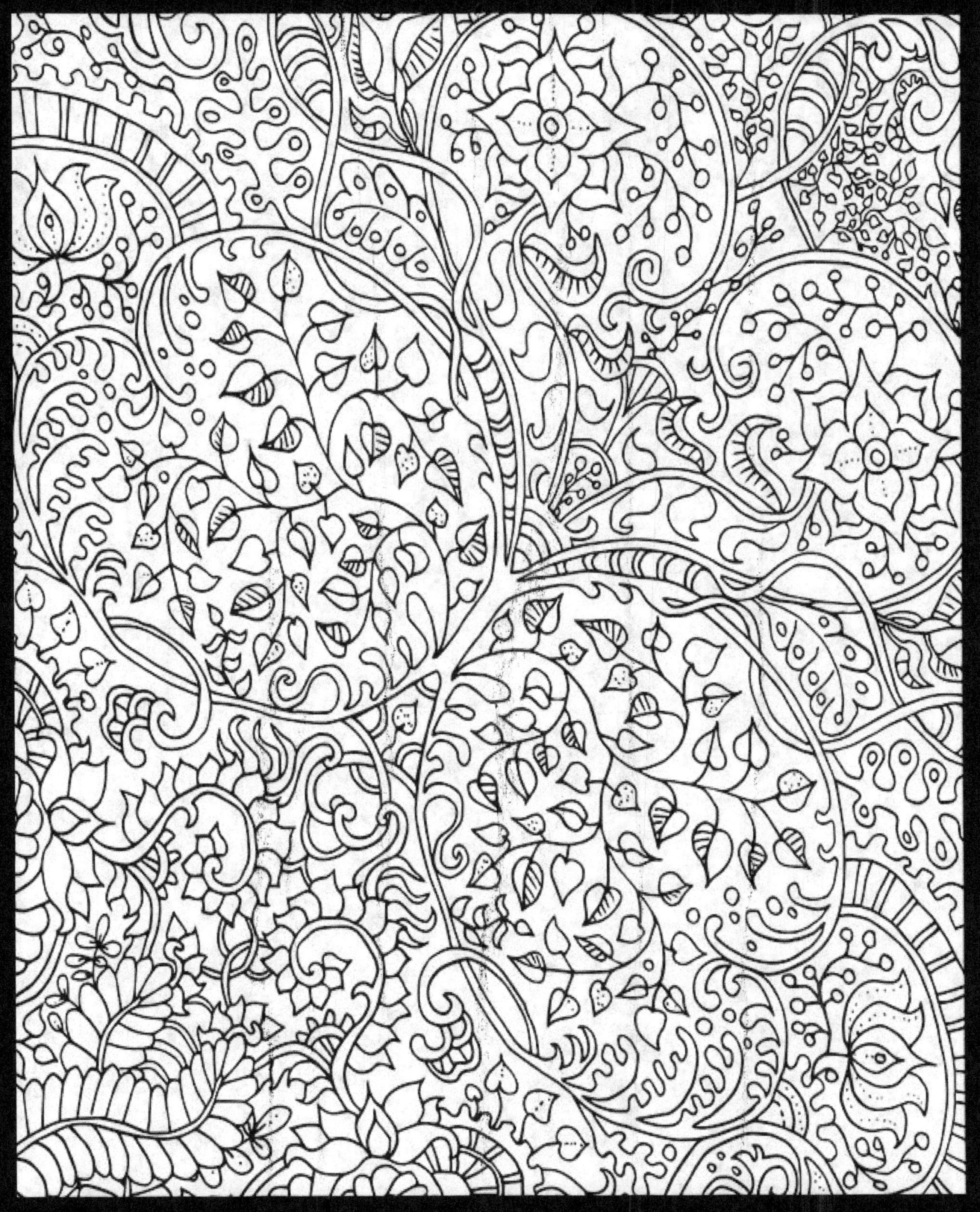

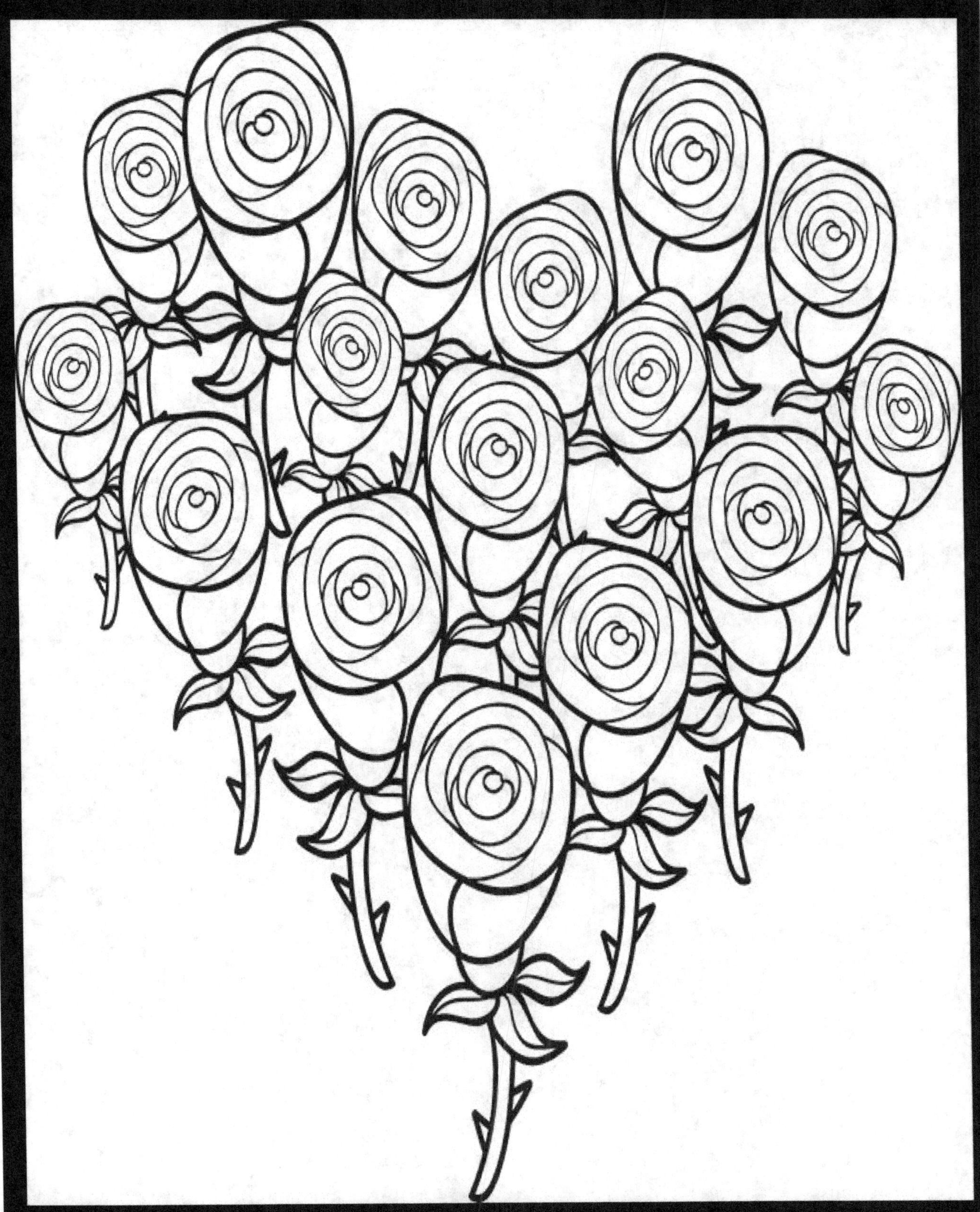

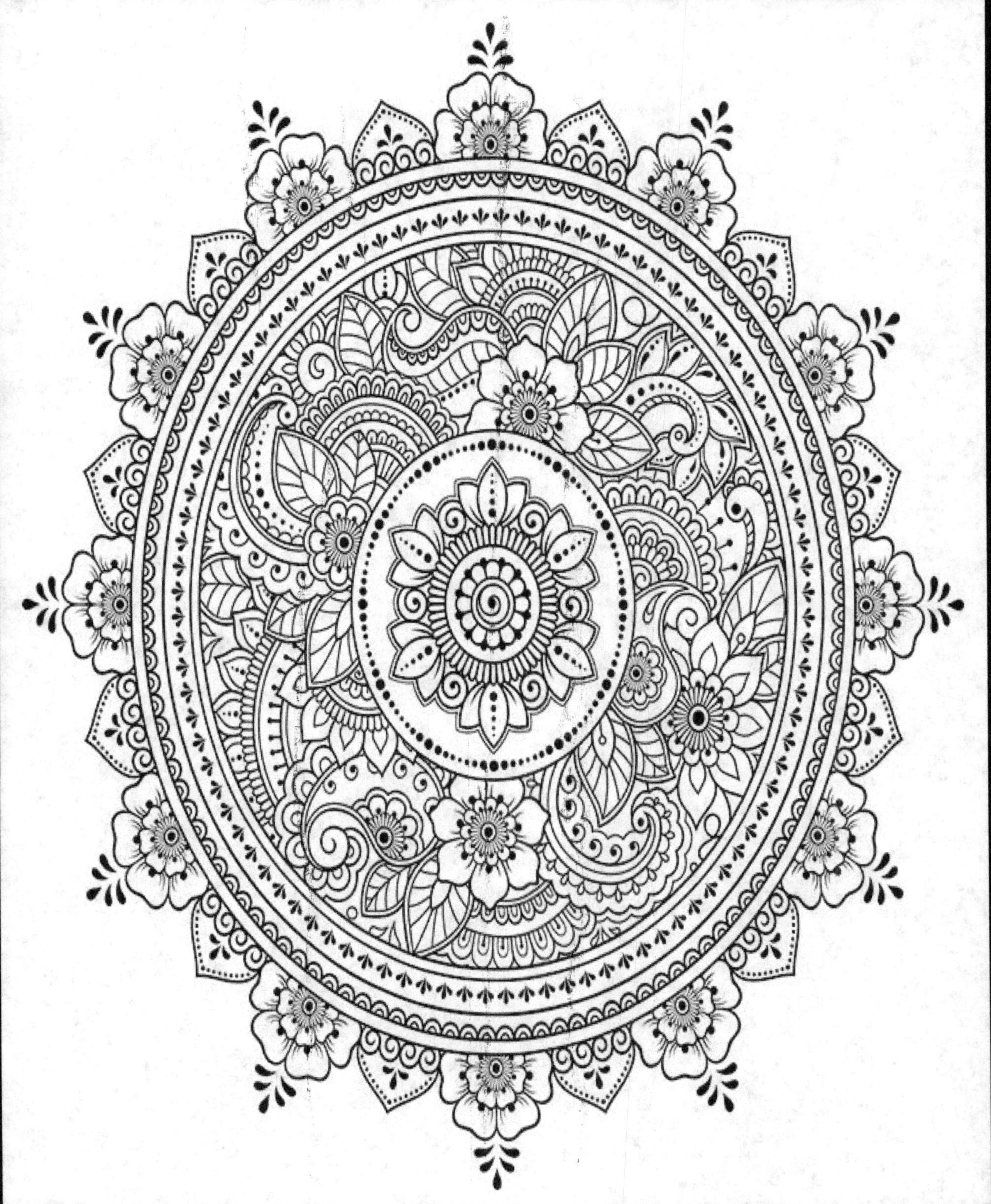

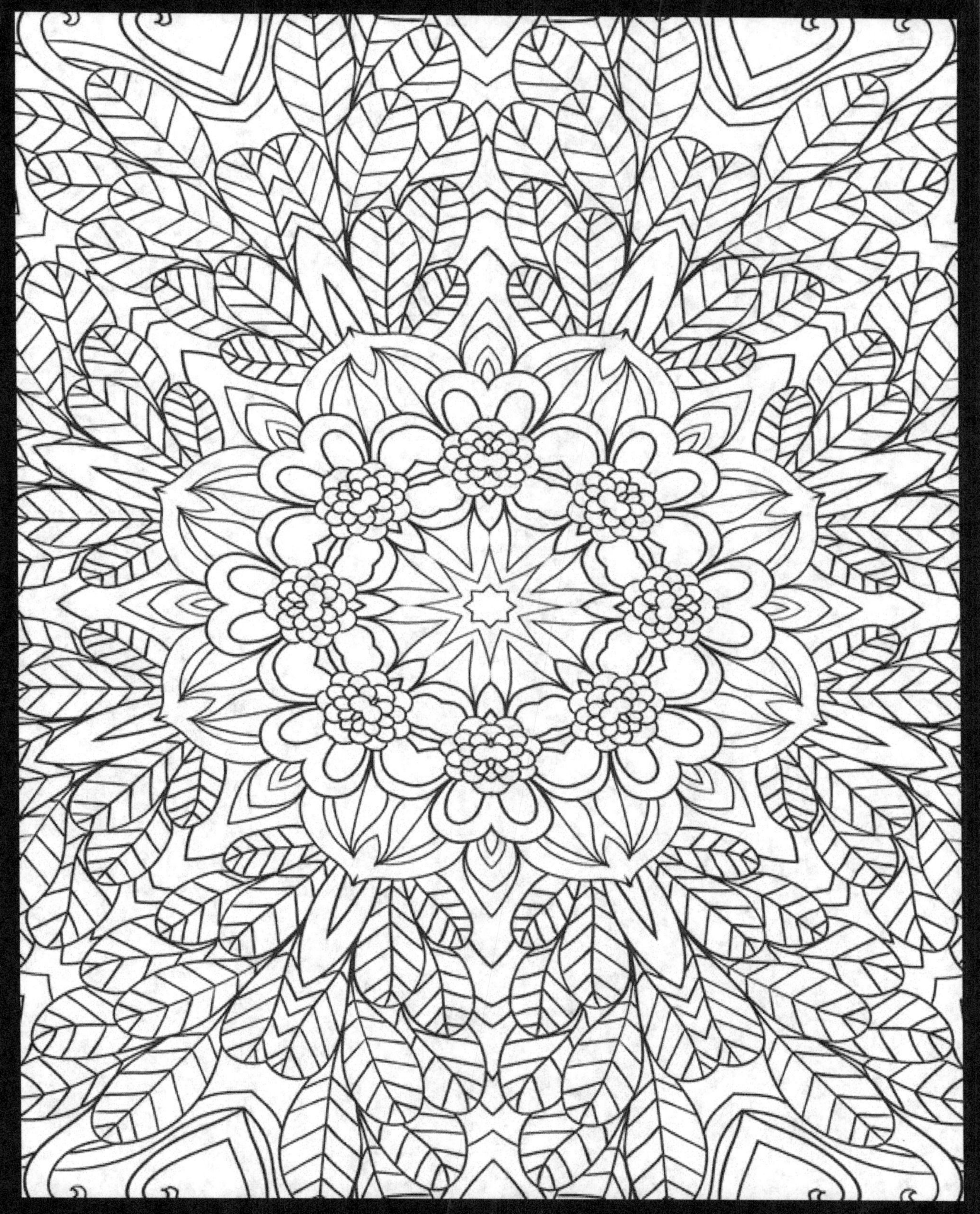

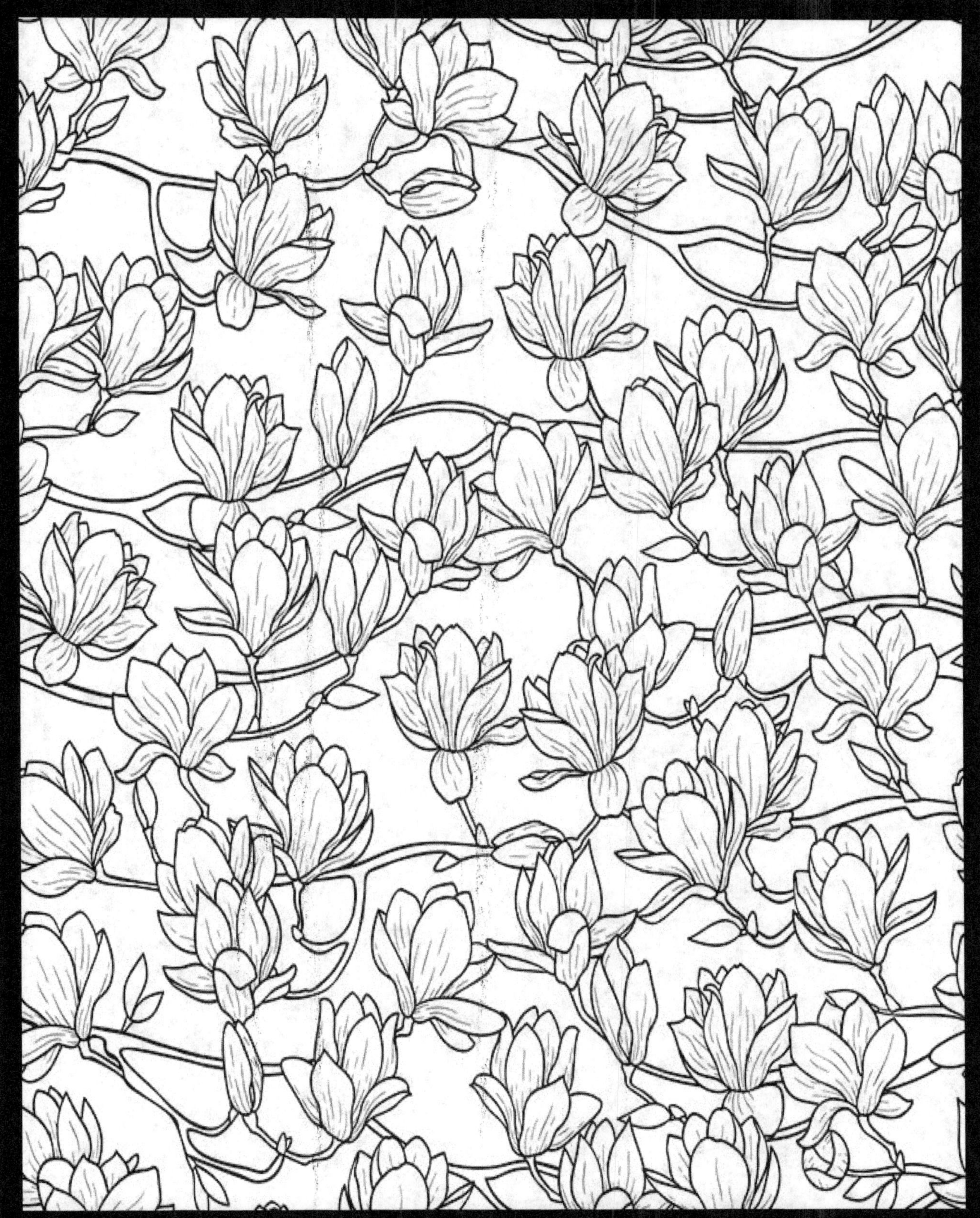

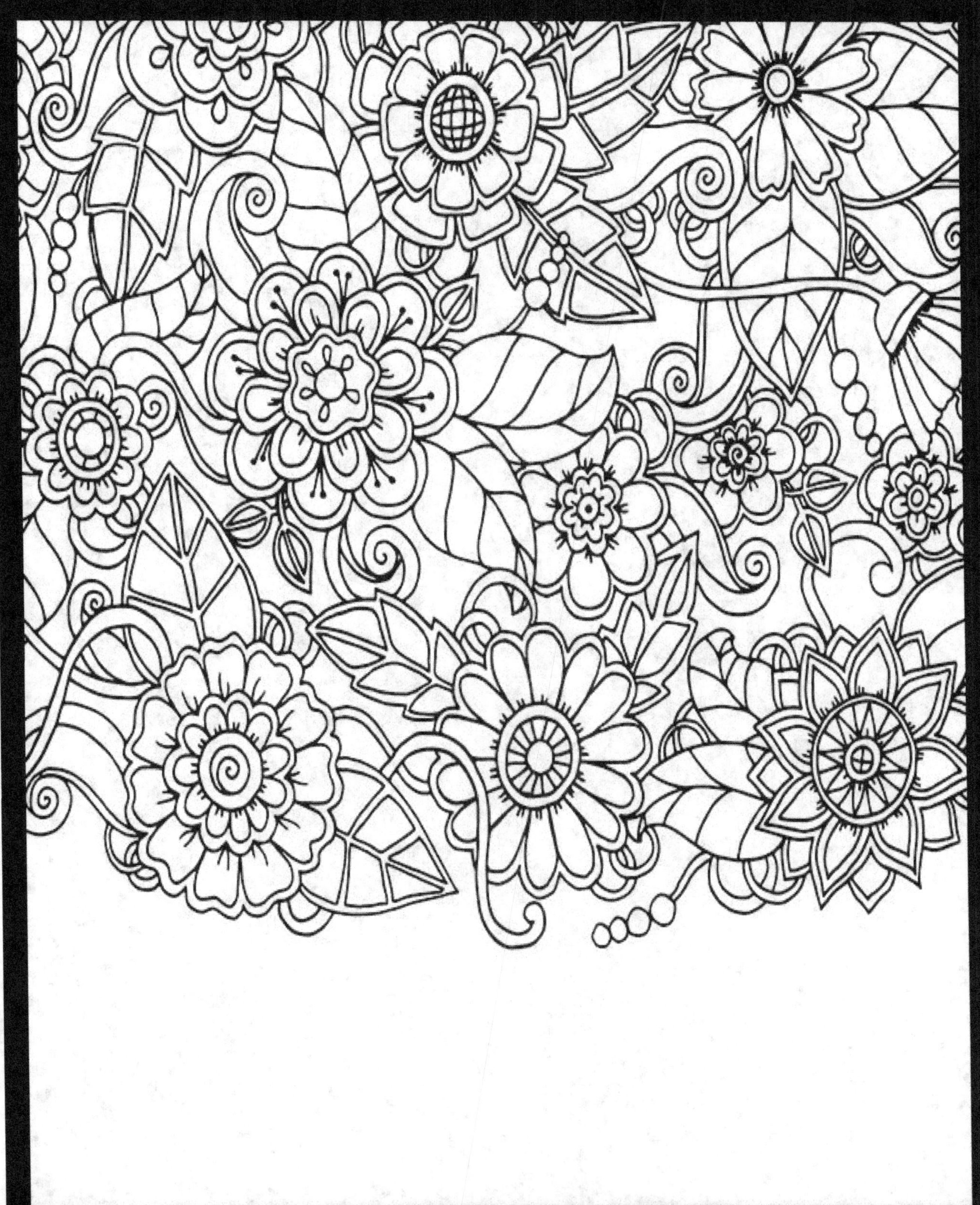

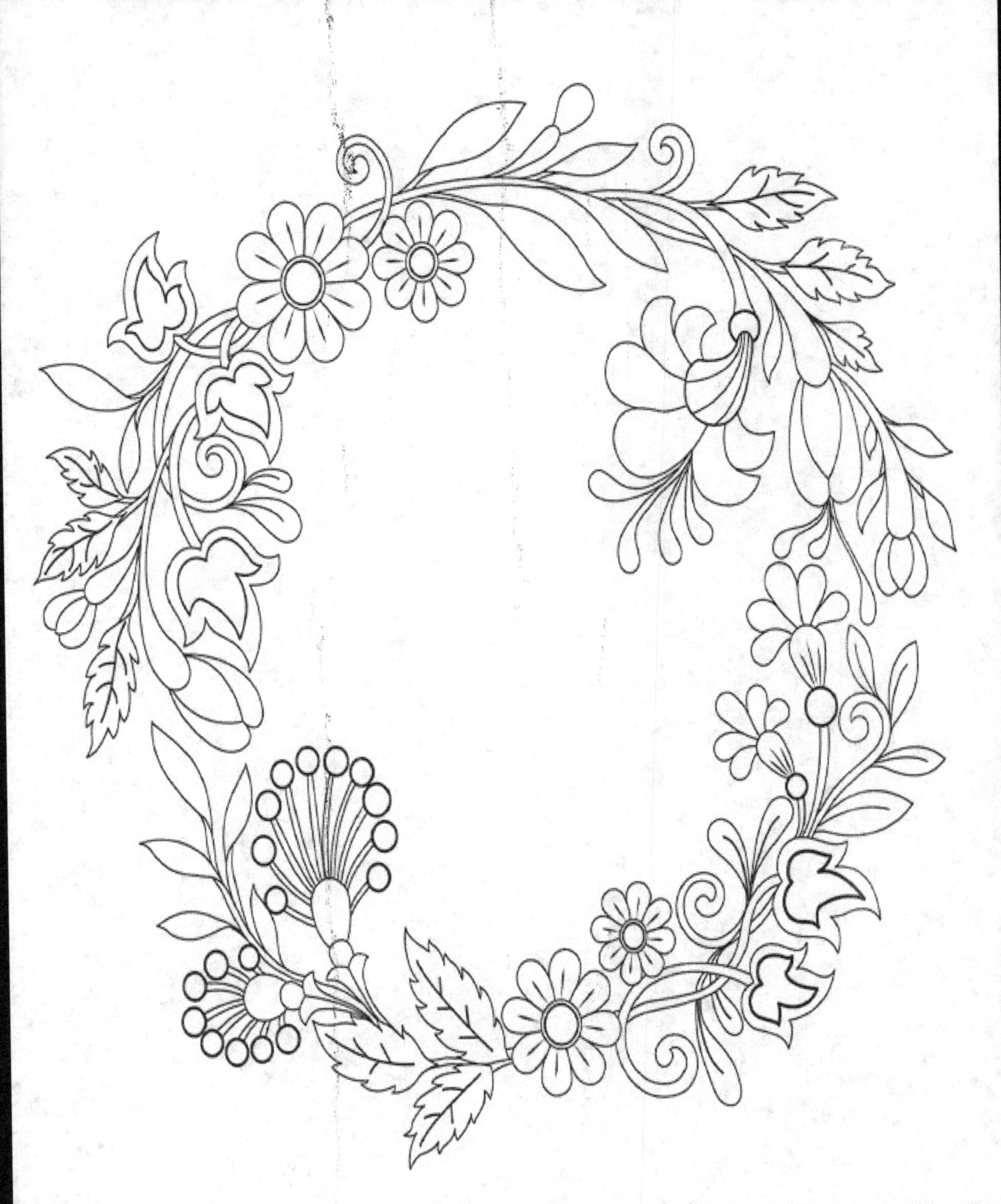

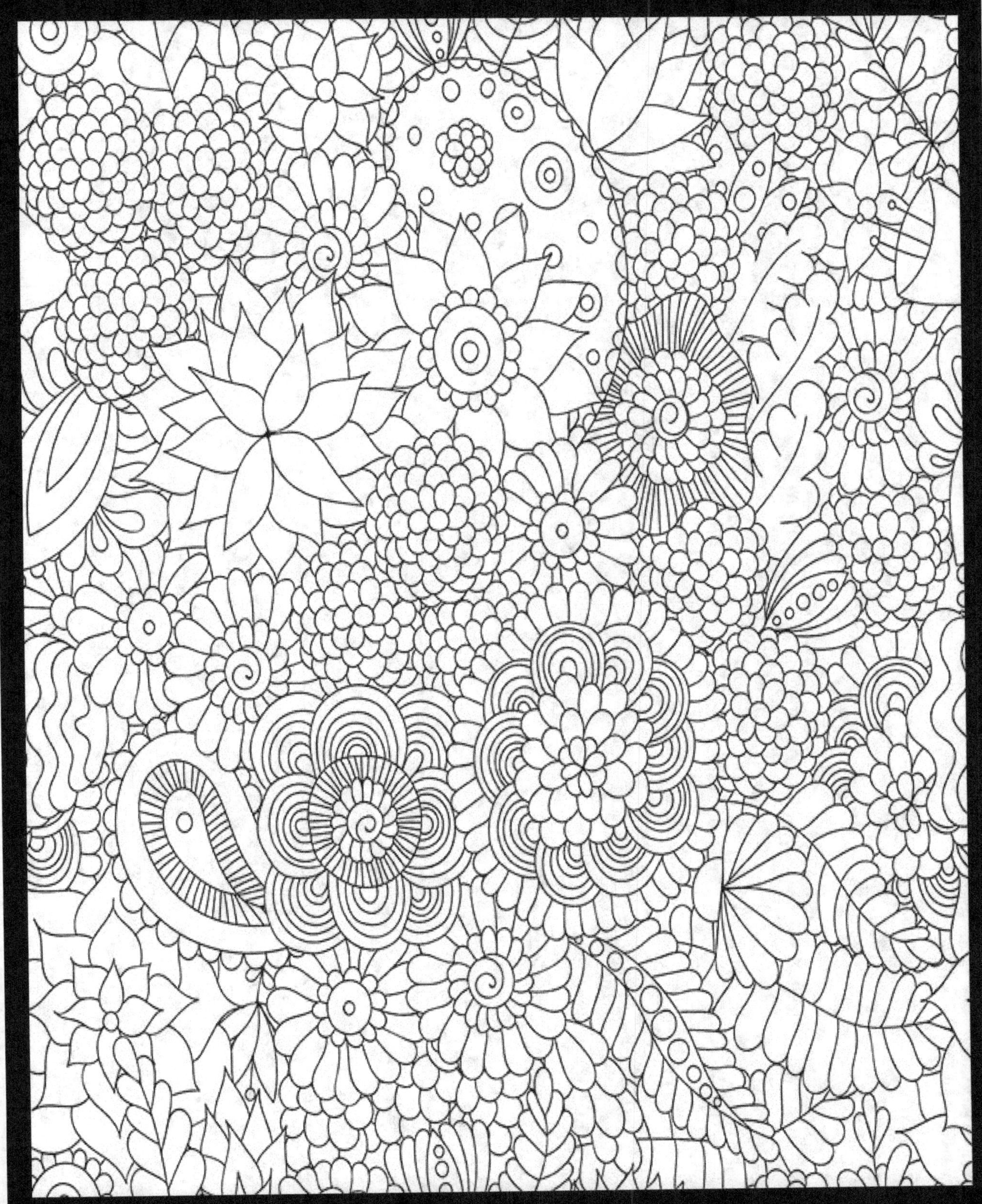

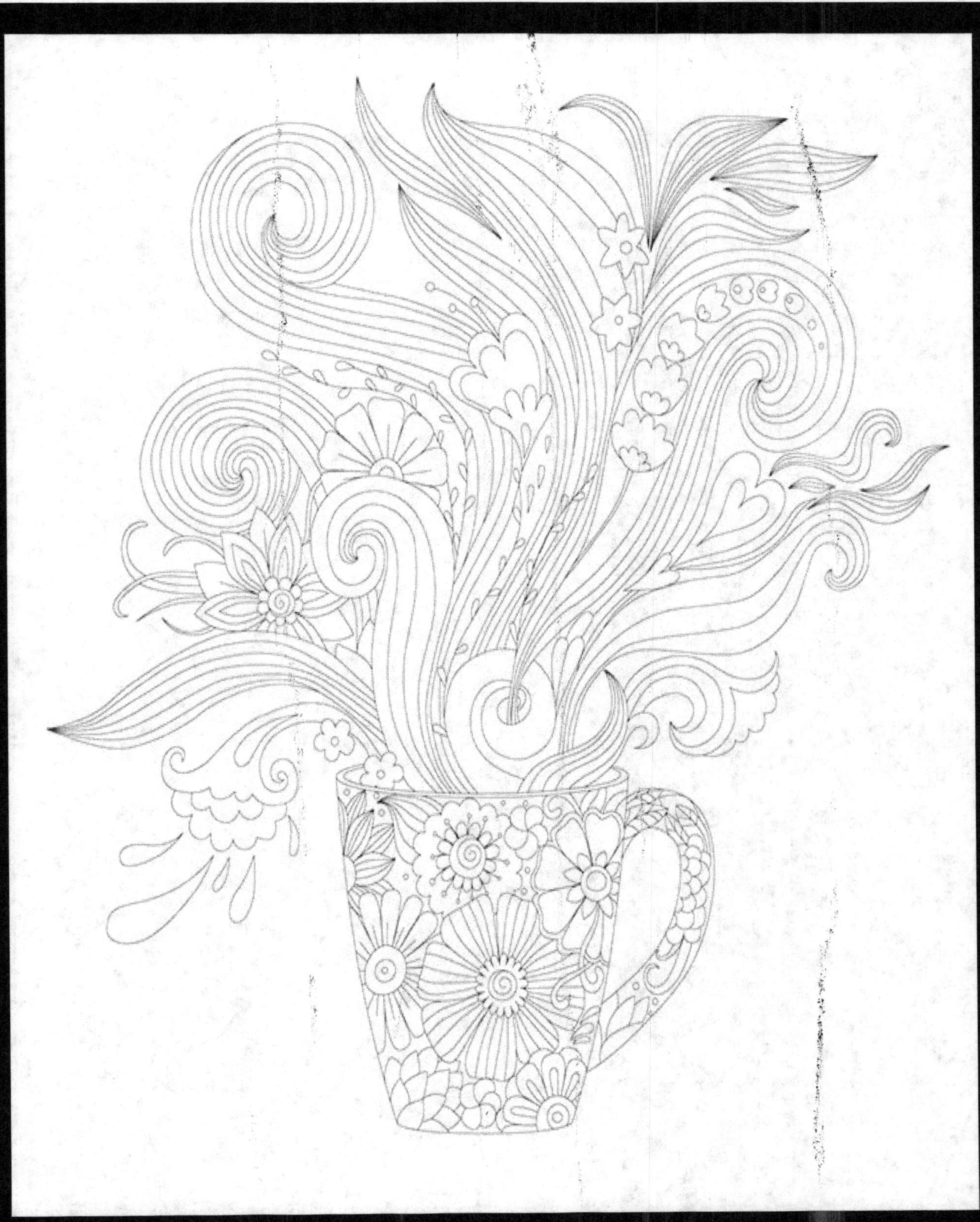

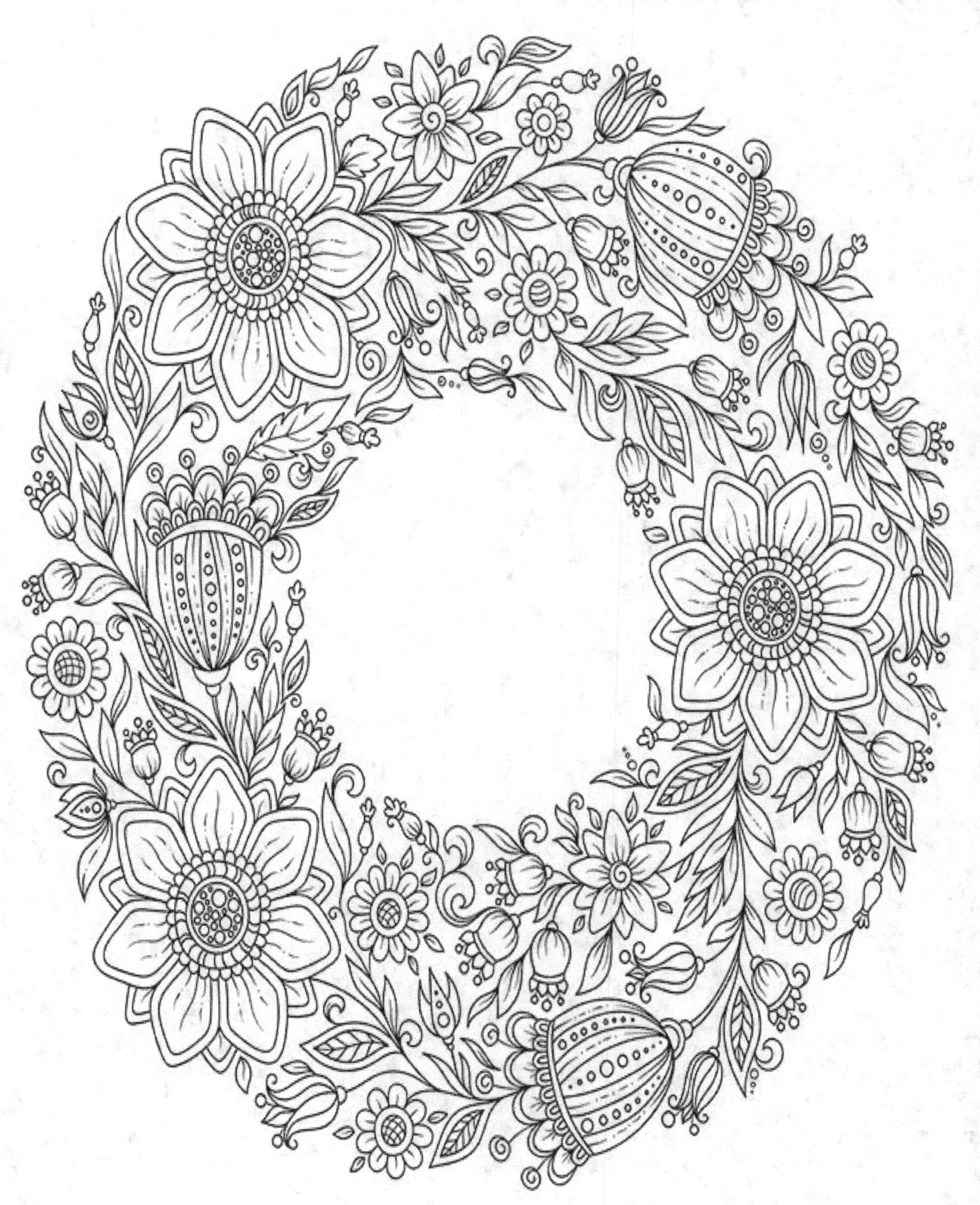

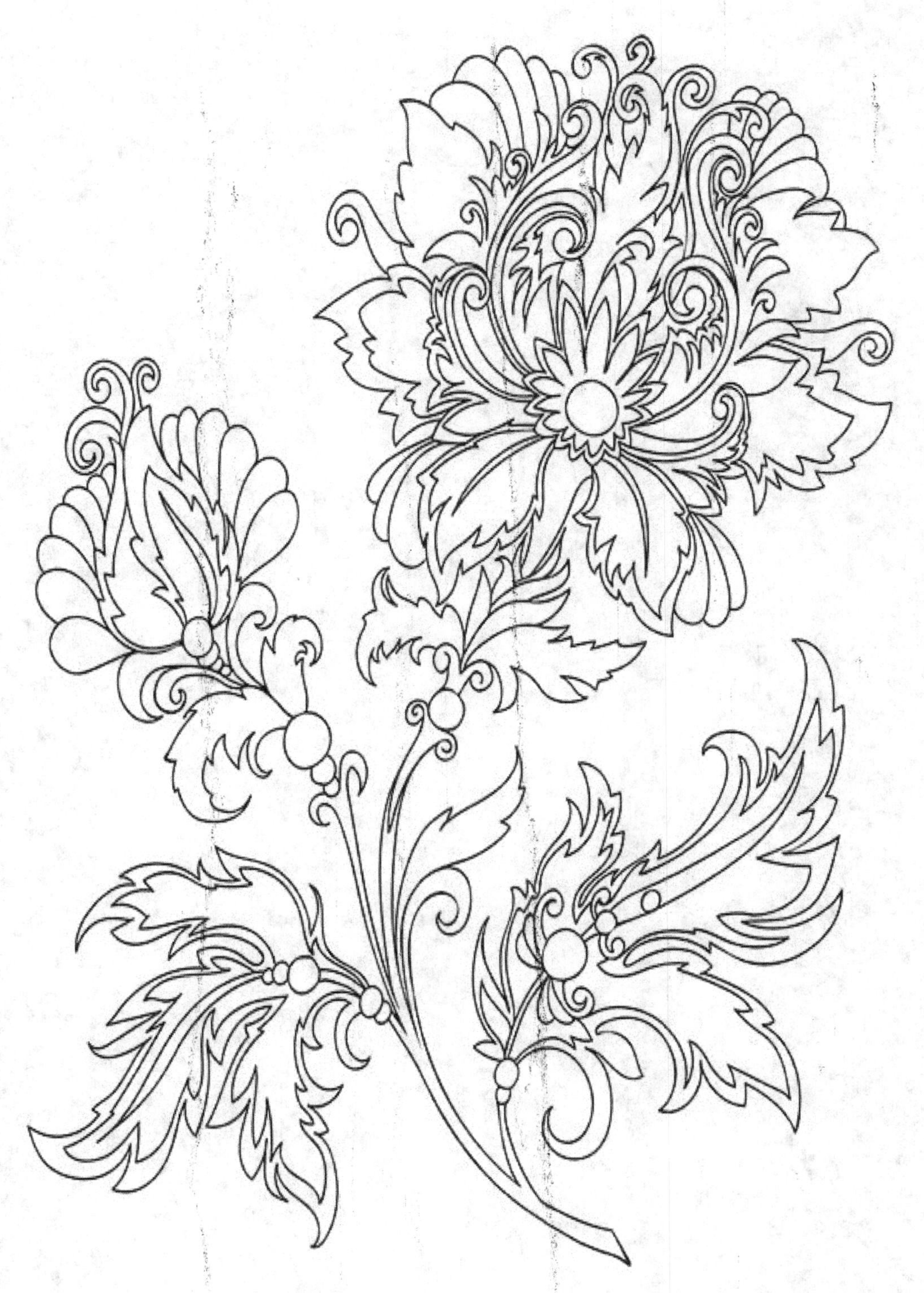

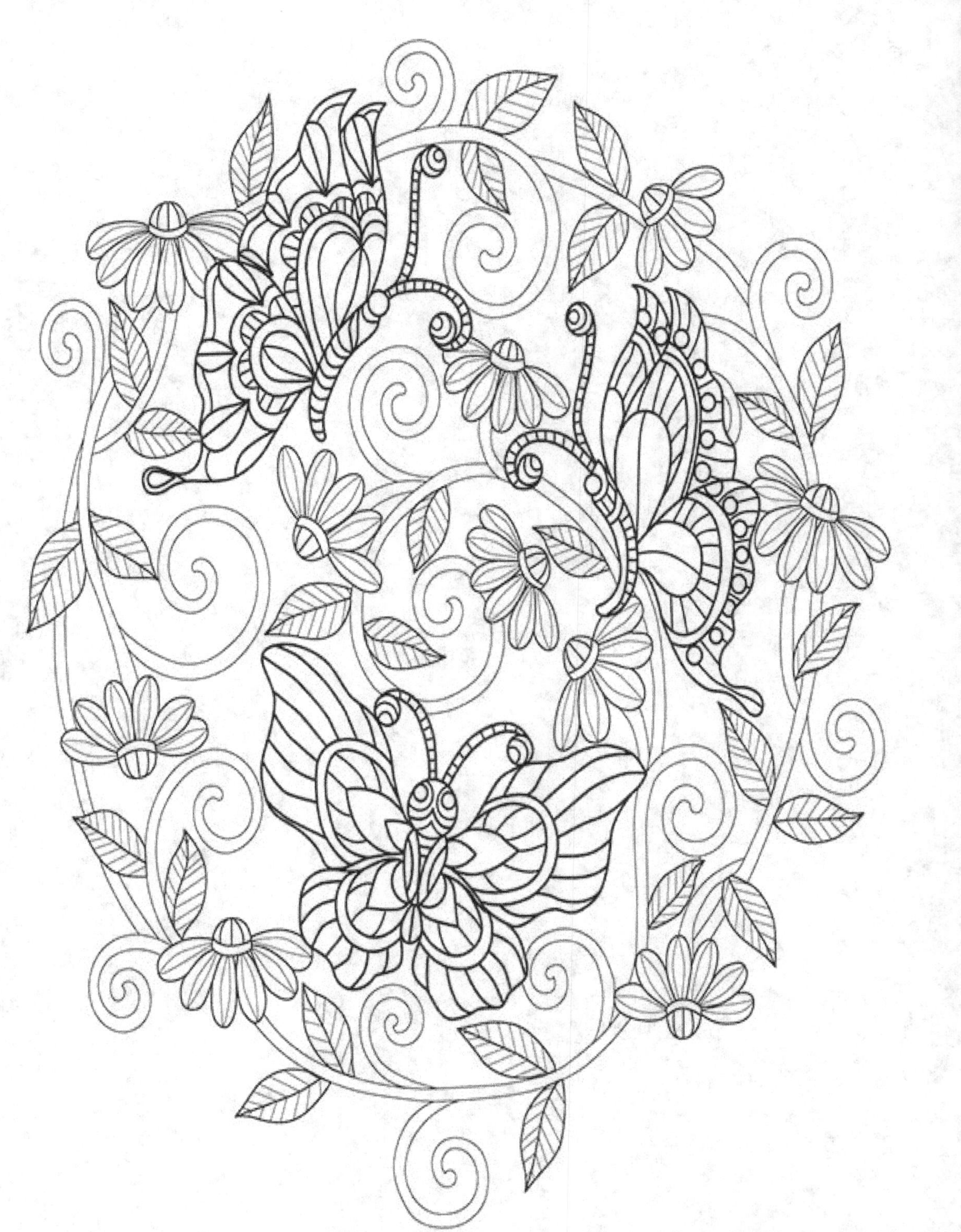

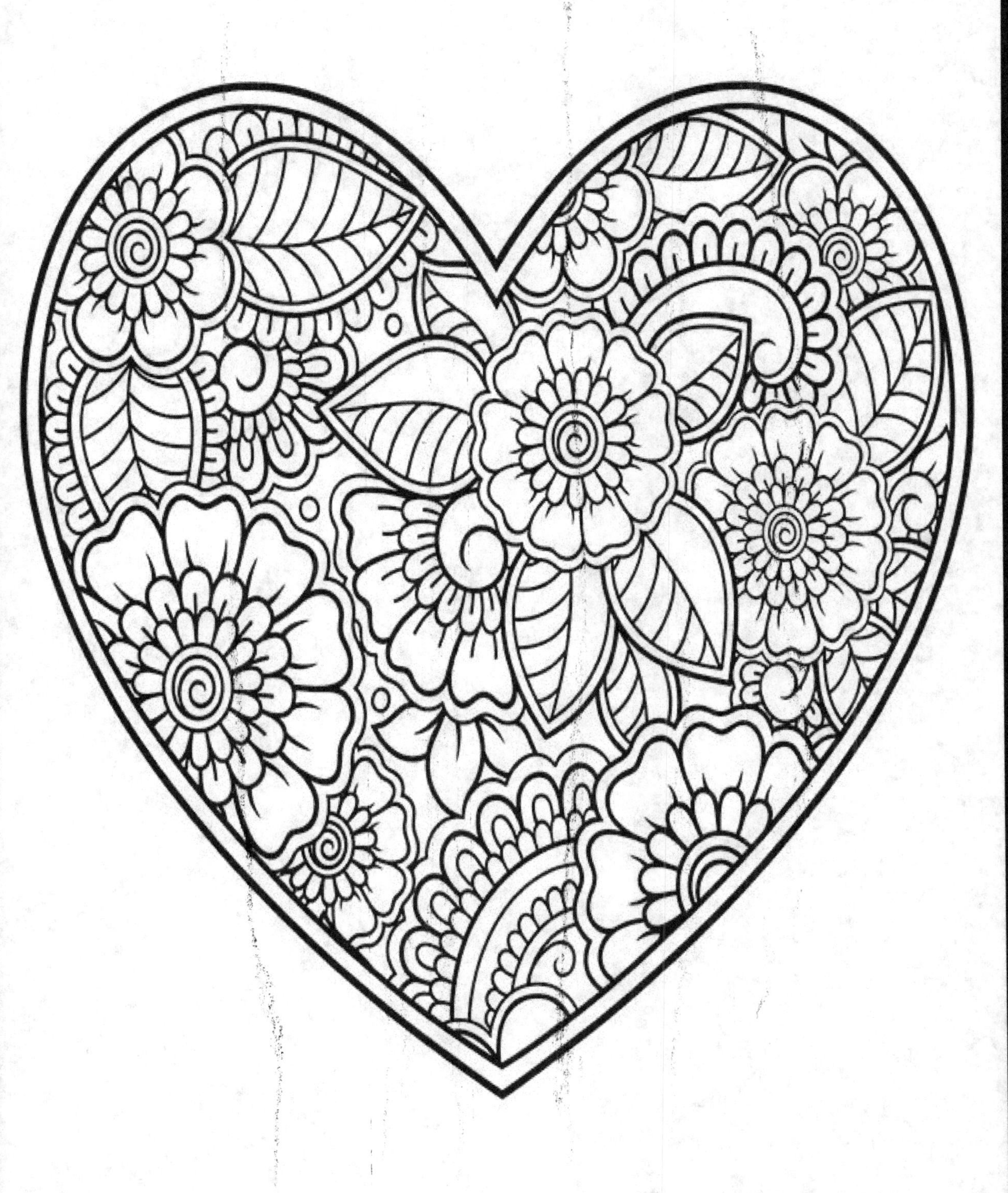

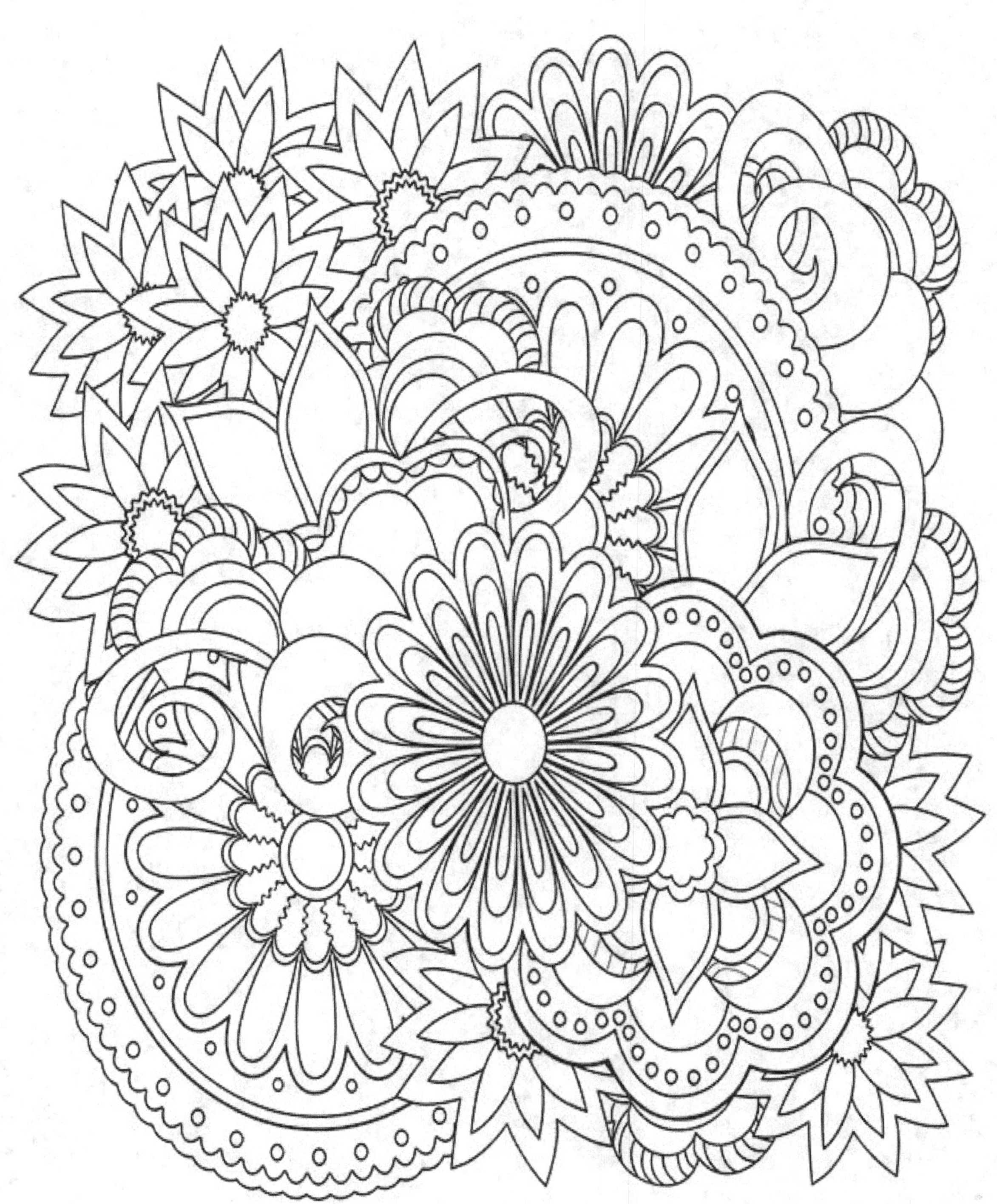

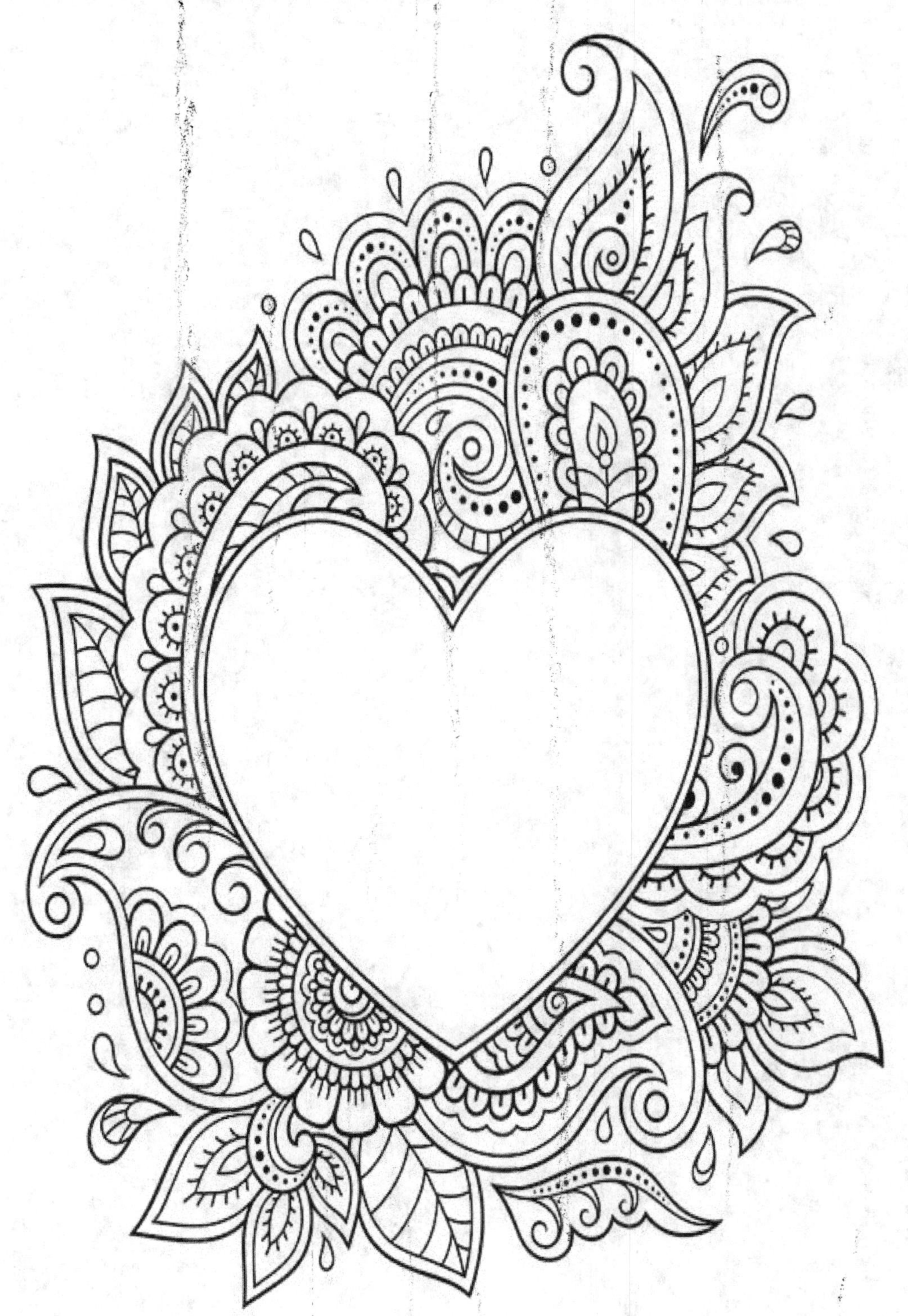

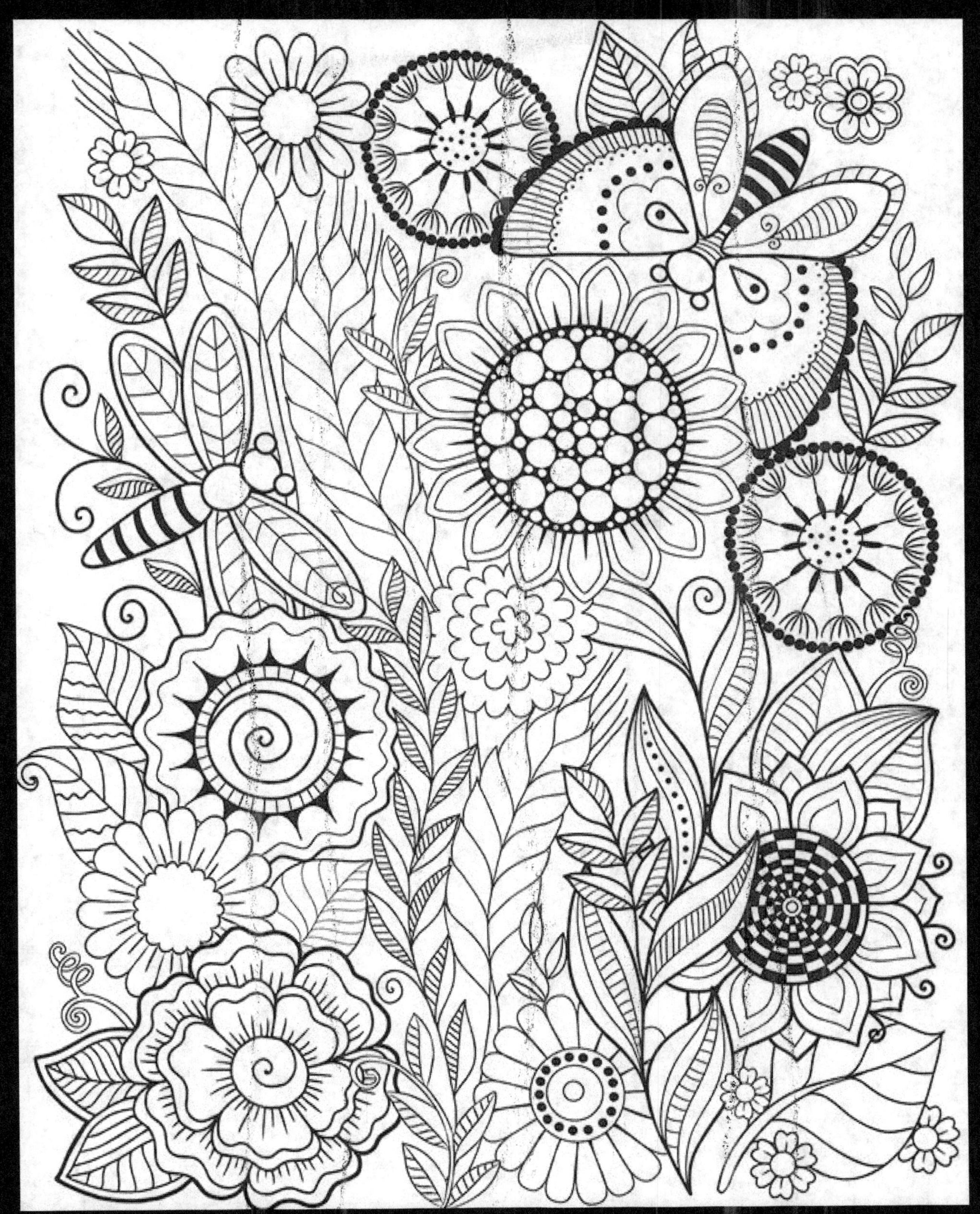

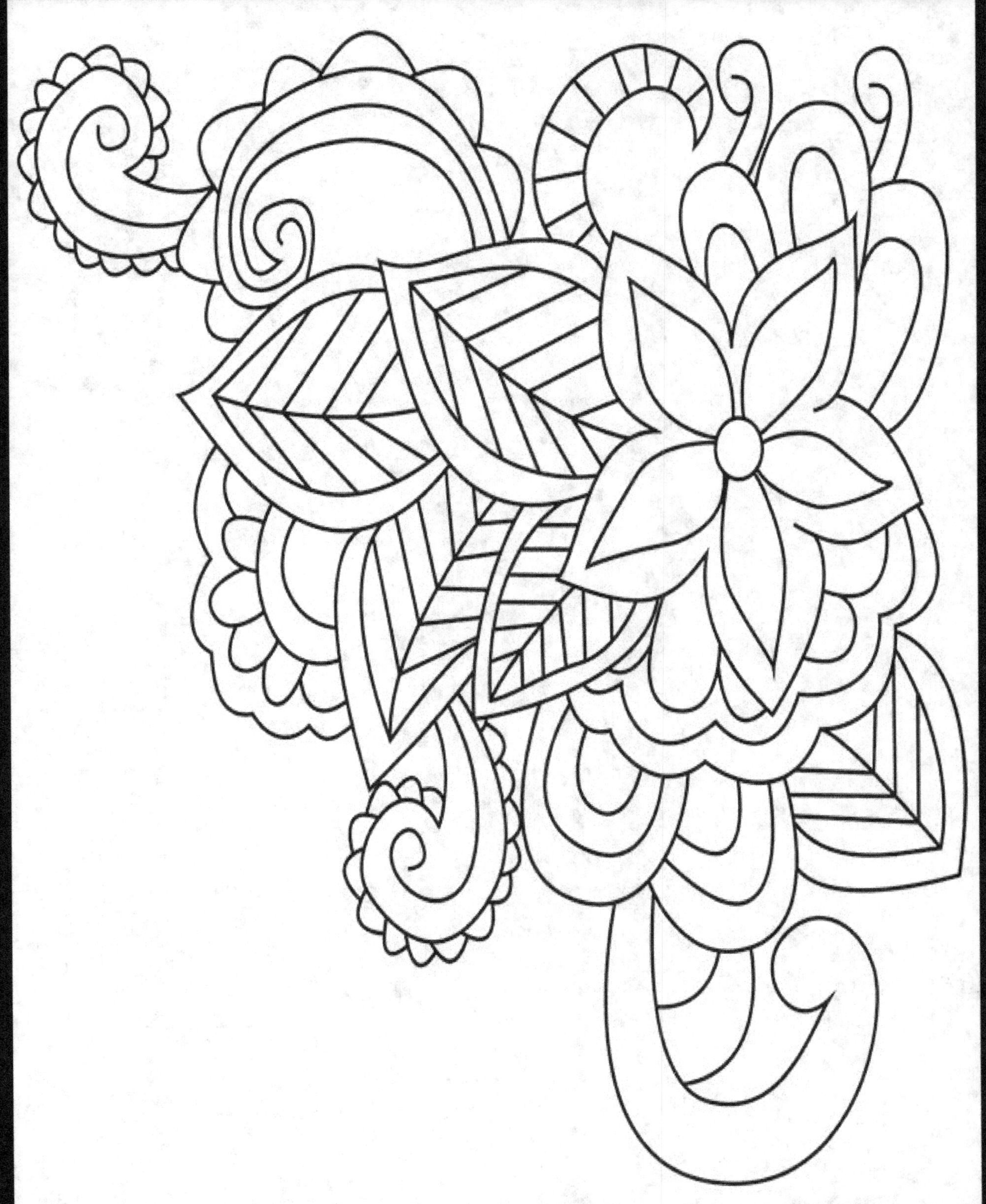

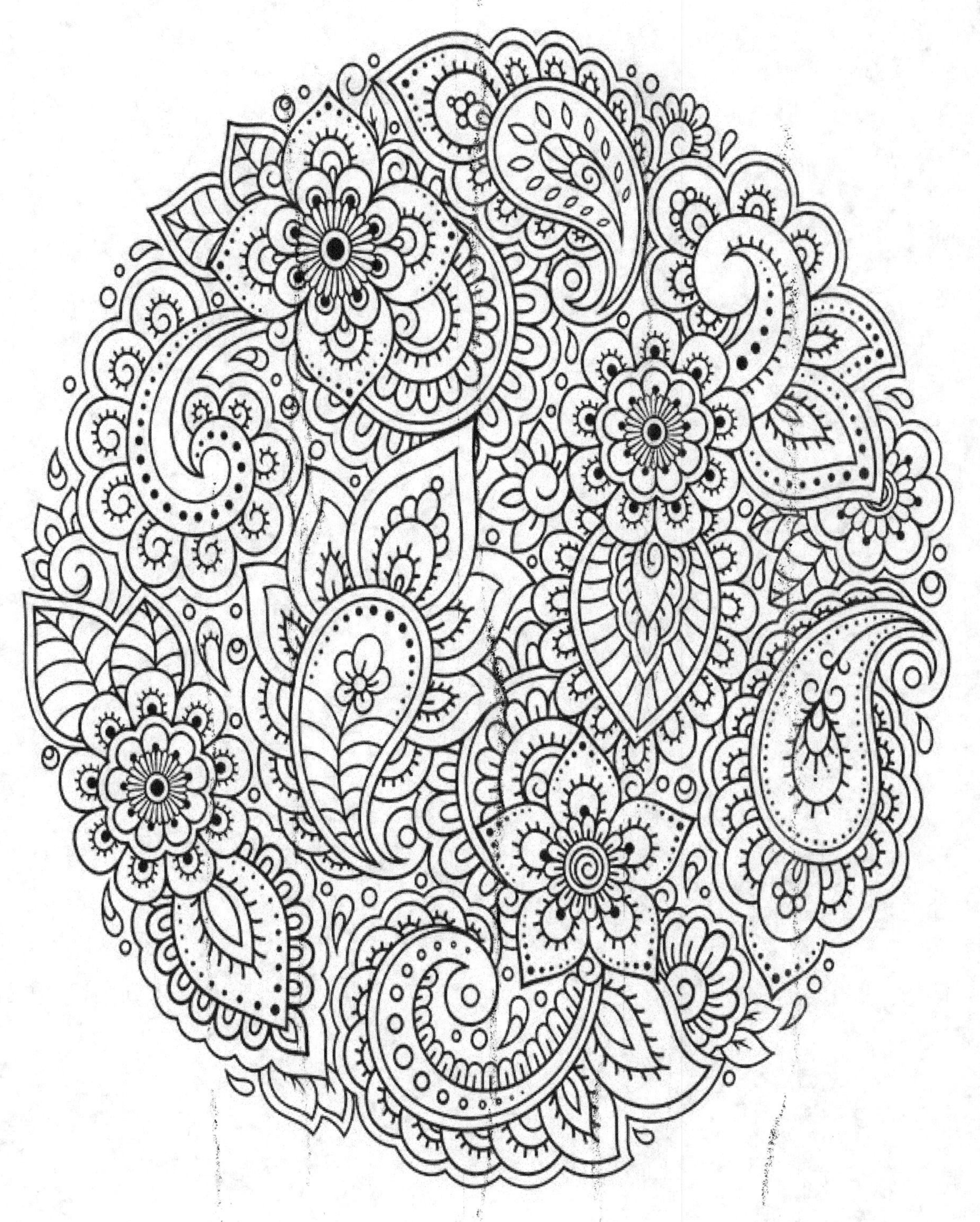

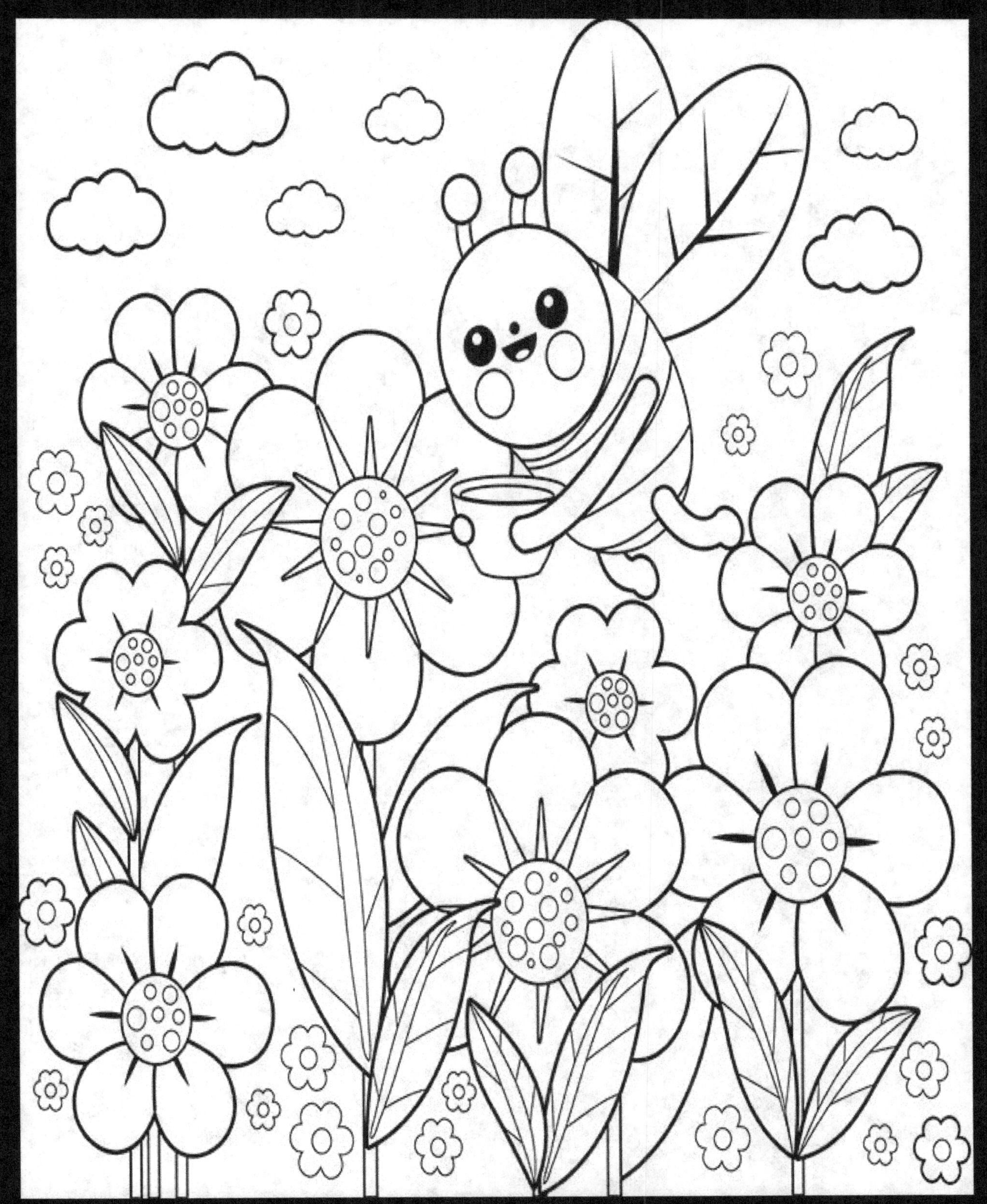

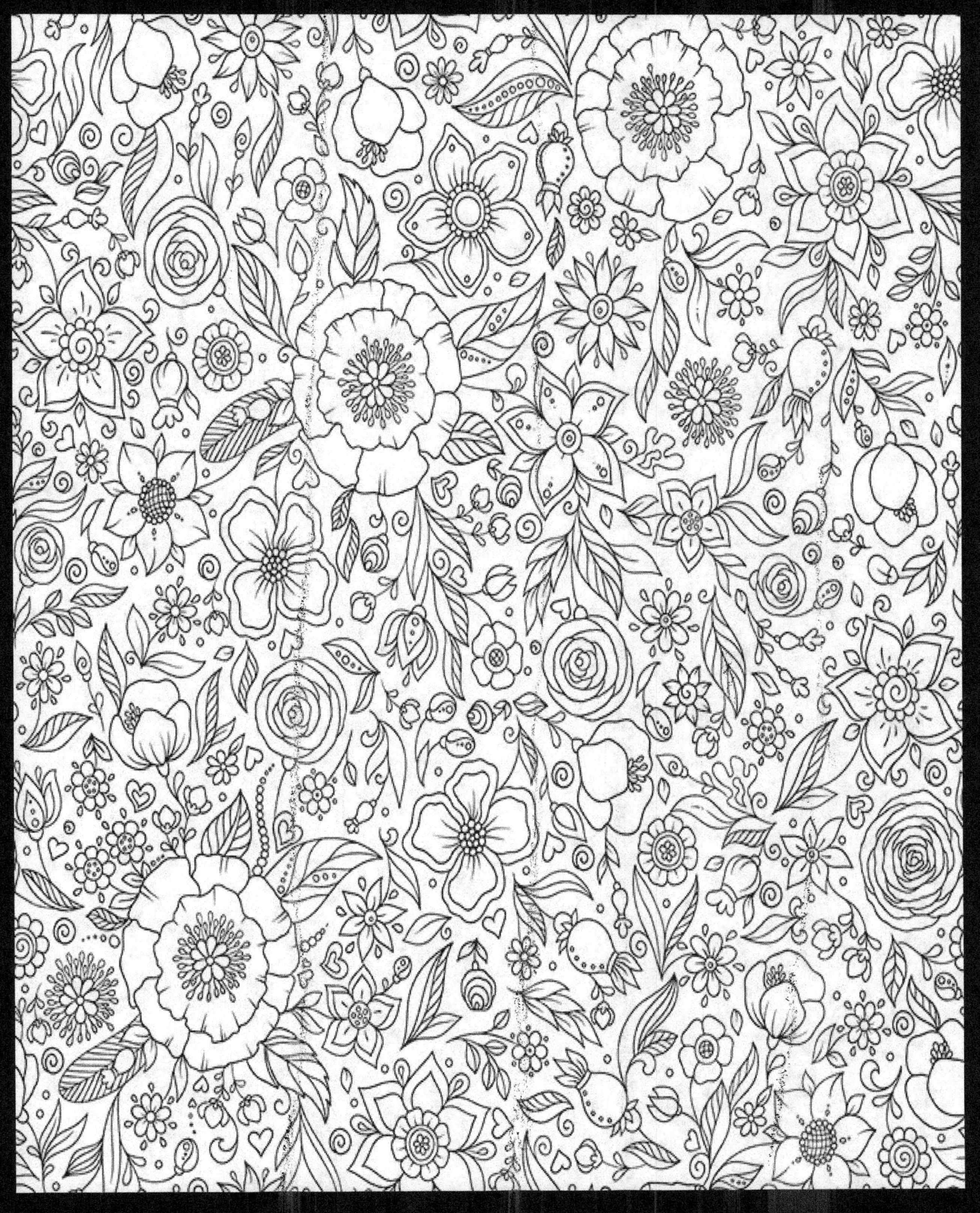

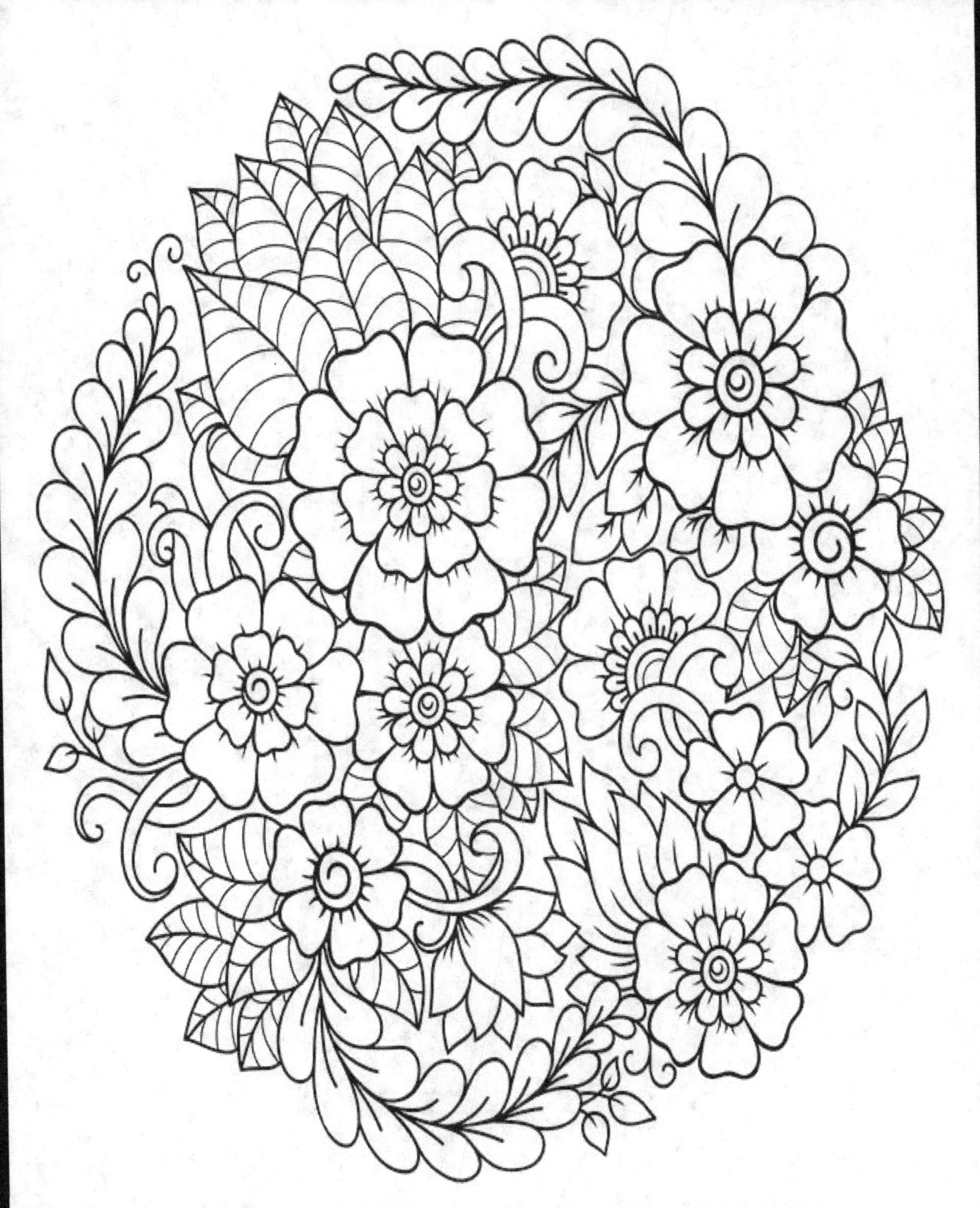

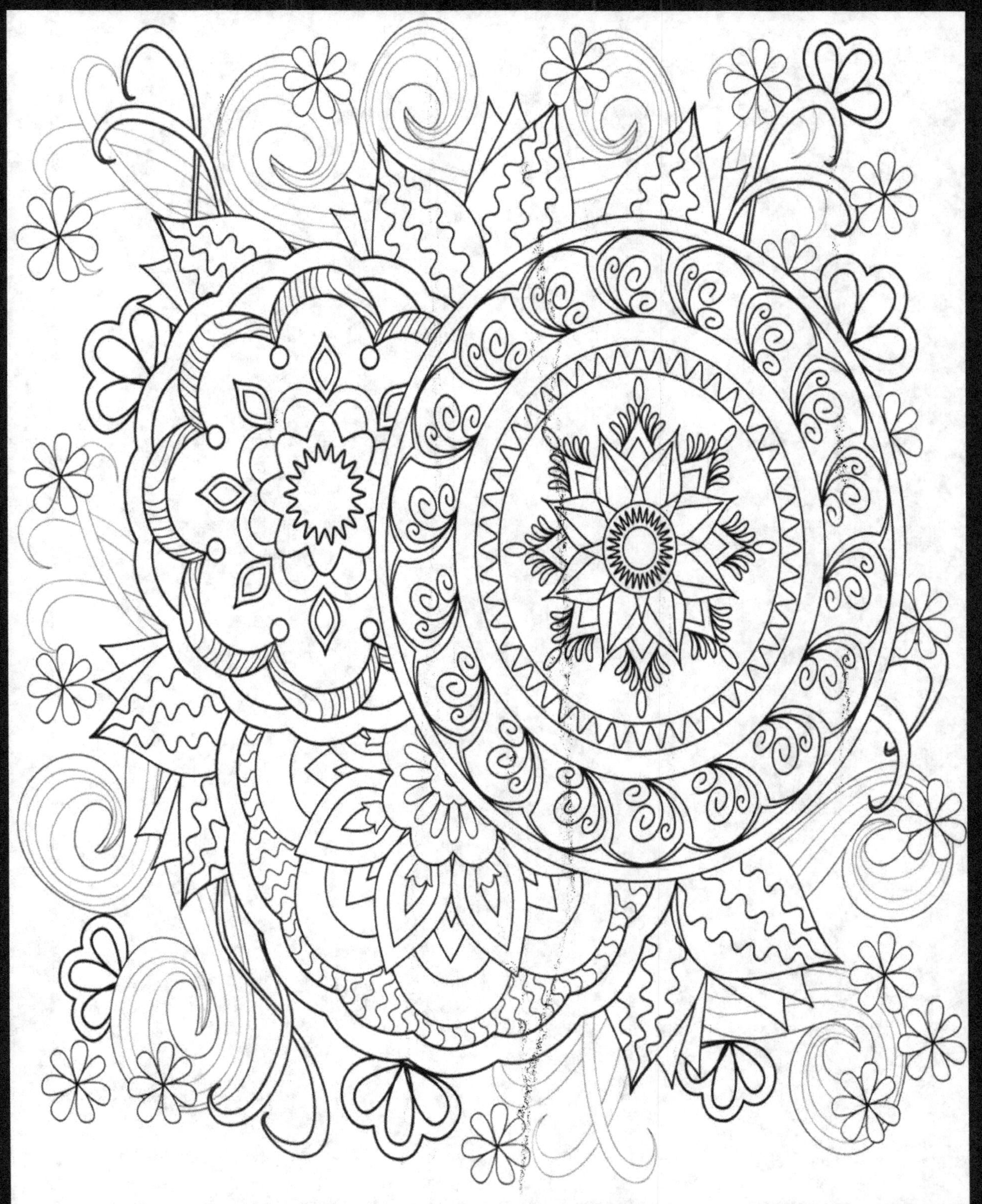

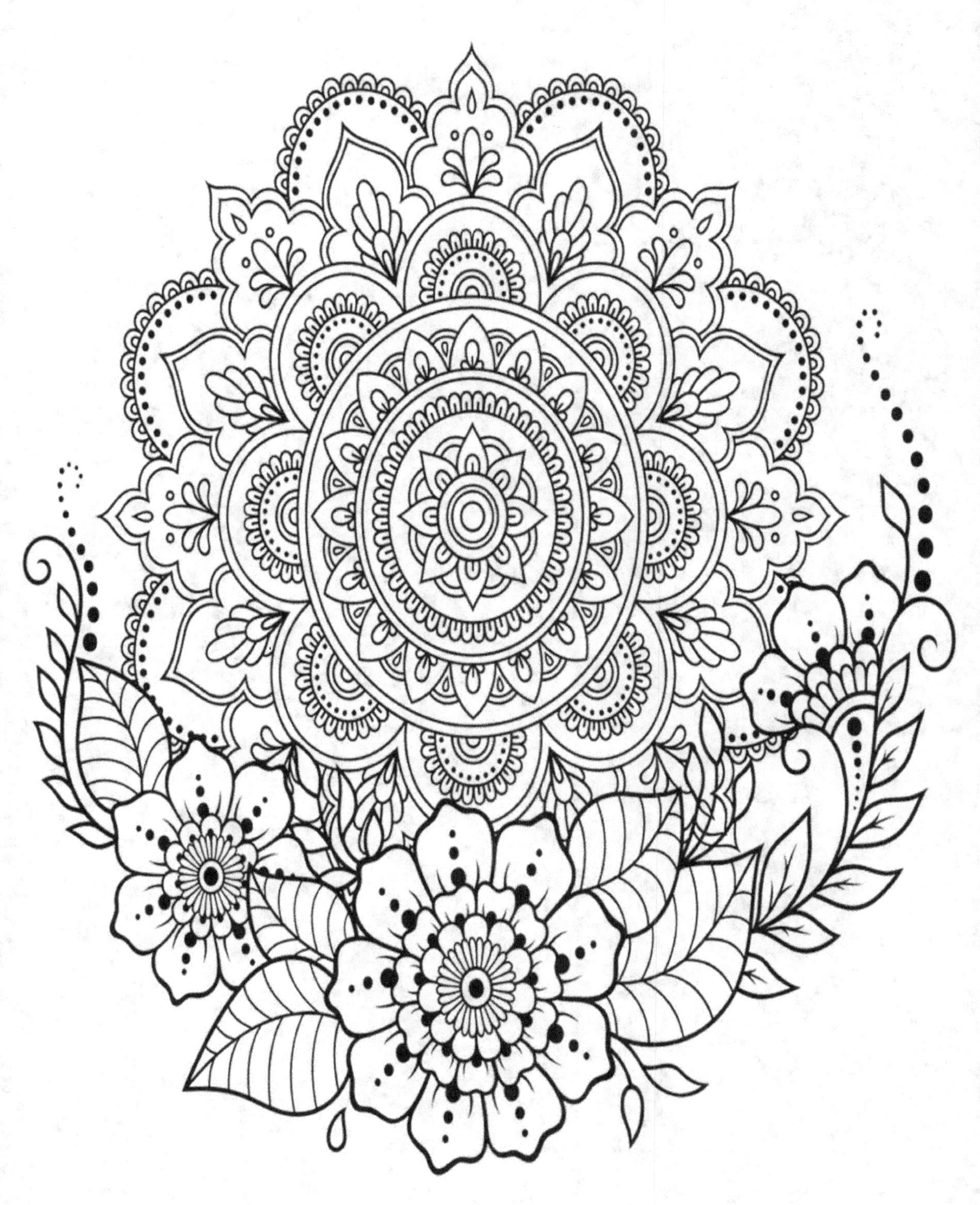

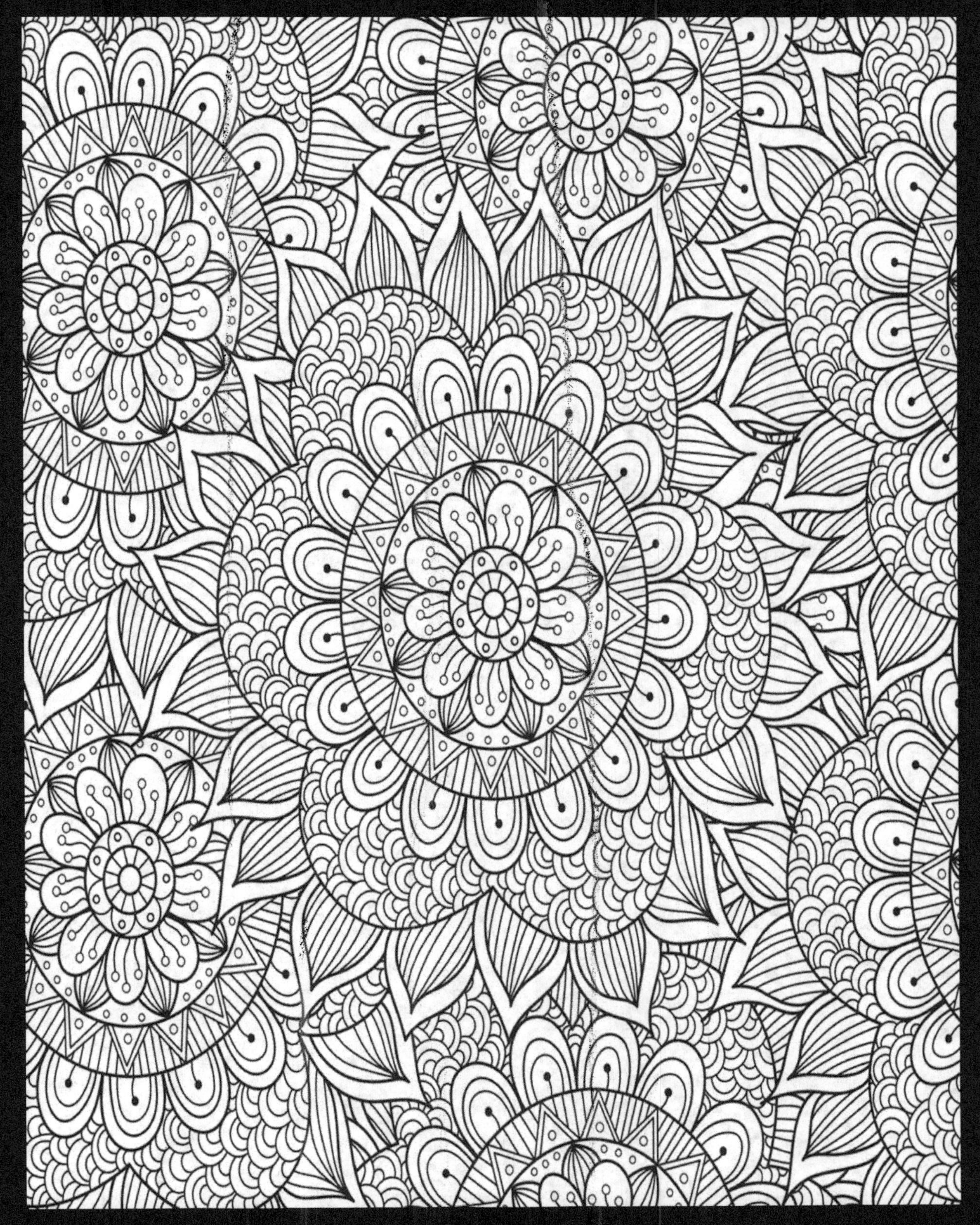

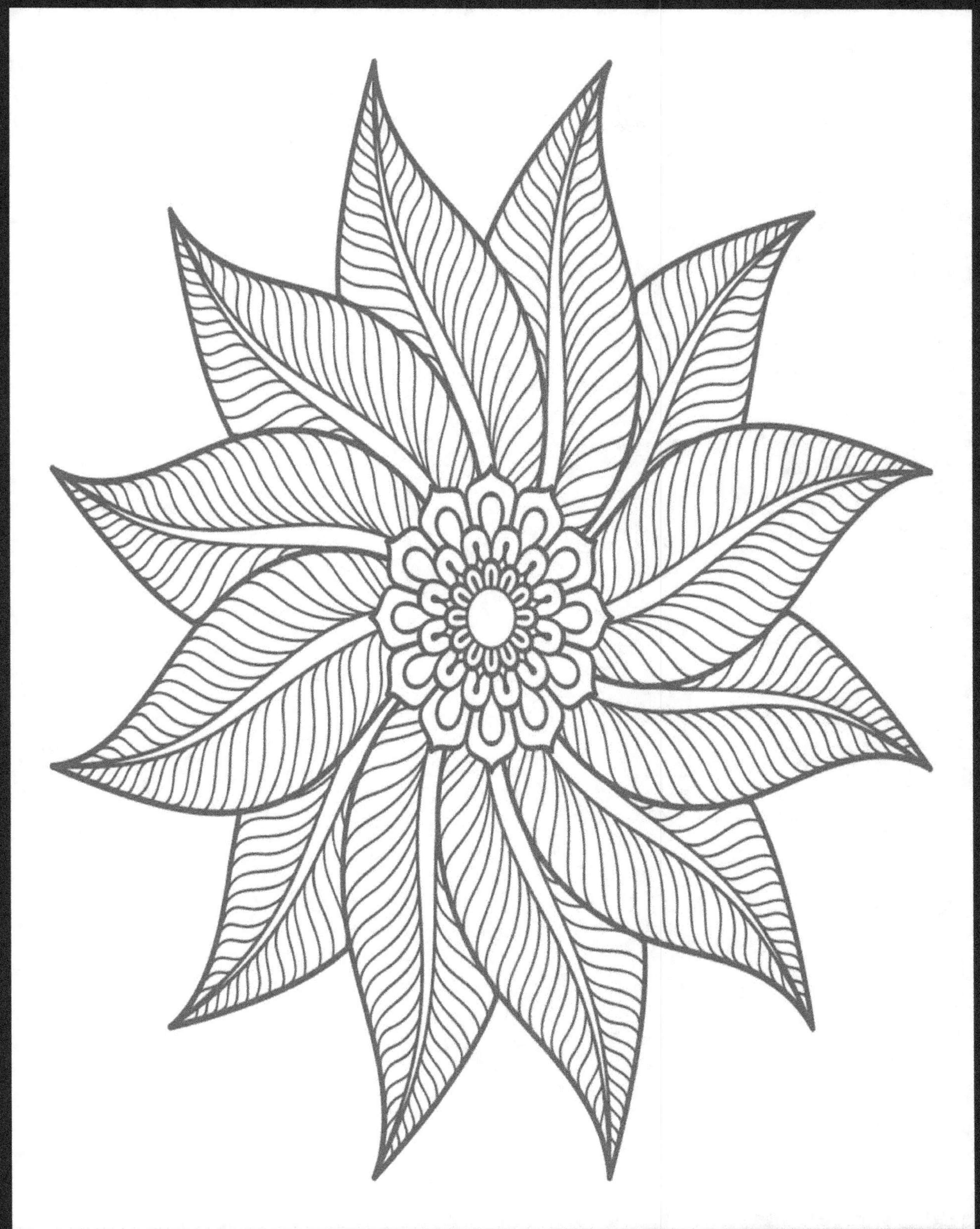